Kiddiwalks IN LONDON

Helen Finch

COUNTRYSIDE BOOKS
NEWBURY BERKSHIRE

First published 2010

COUNTRYSIDE BOOKS
3 Catherine Road
Newbury, Berkshire

To view our complete range of books,
please visit us at
www.countrysidebooks.co.uk

ISBN 978 1 84674 195 1

Designed by Peter Davies, Nautilus Design
Produced through MRM Associates Ltd., Reading
Printed by Information Press, Oxford

Contents

Contents

PUBLISHER'S NOTE

We hope that you obtain considerable enjoyment from this book; great care has been taken in its preparation. Although at the time of publication all routes followed public rights of way or permitted paths, diversion orders can be made and permissions withdrawn.

We cannot, of course, be held responsible for such diversion orders and any inaccuracies in the text which result from these or any other changes to the routes nor any damage which might result from walkers trespassing on private property. We are anxious though that all details covering the walks are kept up to date and would therefore welcome information from readers which would be relevant to future editions.

The simple sketch maps that accompany the walks in this book are based on notes made by the author whilst checking out the routes on the ground. They are designed to show you how to reach the start, to point out the main features of the overall circuit and they contain a progression of numbers that relate to the paragraphs of the text.

Introduction

It all started with my husband. When he decided to train to become a London taxi driver, the whole family became involved. 'The Knowledge' can be a very solitary and focused thing to learn, so over the next five years we all embarked on regular visits to London. It was while we were pounding the city streets that our eldest son started to connect the buildings, statues and historical facts with what he was learning at school. This gave me the idea that if I put together walks reflecting the subjects that children encounter in their classrooms, these trips would be even more beneficial. With the invention of the internet it is so easy to type in a topic and get an array of answers. However, there is nothing like seeing things for oneself to bring pictures or text in a book to life – children absorb information and I hope that this collection of walks will help to make the process enjoyable for them.

There is something to tempt even the most 'indoor loving' youngster. Each route is between 1 to just over 2 miles and will take approximately 2 hours to walk at a leisurely place, with plenty of munch stops and opportunities along the way to just run around and let off steam. The walks are aimed at any age of child (even us bigger ones!) as I have put in something for everyone – and where the route is suitable for a pushchair, I have mentioned that too. Additional places of interest have been included so you can plan a whole day's outing if you wish – it is entirely up to you. I have combined parks with historical facts and other walks with topics that are covered by the school curriculum, such as the Great Fire of London, the Tudors, Boudicca and Florence Nightingale.

There is a short introduction at the start of every walk, together with useful information on the facilities available and transport links. Sketch maps are also provided for each walk but it would probably be useful to also have a street map of London to hand. I have incorporated ideas within the routes that will get the kids thinking and perhaps wanting to learn more; some even have an I-Spy element so you can play along too!

There are royal parks to discover and special events are often held in them so it is worth checking their website (www.royalparks.org.uk) before you visit to see what is going on. You will find museums for hands-on learning, hidden squares, an inner-city farm and an oasis of a nature

AREA MAP SHOWING THE LOCATIONS OF THE WALKS

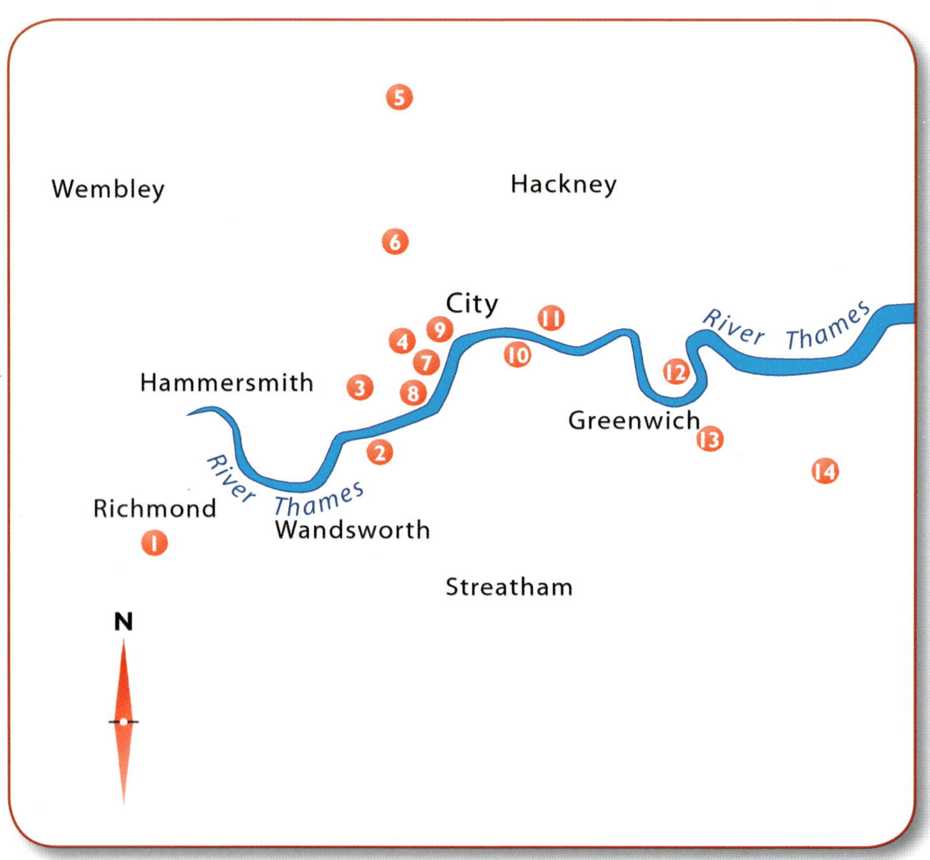

reserve amid busy streets. Walk in the footsteps of Dickens. Travel by river, as Henry VIII would have done, to Greenwich and then stand astride the Meridian Line. Take yourself back to the days before motor vehicles. Get up high for views over London or walk freely with farm animals. Take a trip along the canal whilst watching the wildlife and be entertained in Covent Garden. So grab your 'little sponges' and take them on a journey through a wonderful city. And even if you are a resident or work in the area, you can see things through the eyes of a tourist. Take 'holiday' photos – and when you look back, remember what a great day you all had. We may not all want to study to become a London taxi driver, but it is extraordinary how much we don't know about our capital city. And most importantly, HAVE FUN!

Helen Finch

ACKNOWLEDGEMENTS

I would like to thank, in the first instance, Thomas and Luke who tested out all the kiddiwalks, and my Mum, who walked the Fire of London route with us, despite being asked by the children if she was around during 1666. Thanks, too, to Mollie and Hilary Barker who enjoyed a day out in Regent's Park (and the shopping that followed), and Ryan Gadsden who had a fun time learning about famous people. Also other friends who recommended places to visit and helped with detailed information: Rose Gladdish and Tiffany Mutti, Linda Smith and Mrs Thorn. Gratitude goes to my patient husband Roy who drew all the original maps for me and enjoyed the walks just as much as the children. Also I would like to mention the staff at the *Golden Hinde*, Royal Naval College, Camley Street Nature Reserve, the Canal Museum, Alexandra Palace, the *Cutty Sark*, Mudchute Farm, the Royal Albert Hall, Tower Hamlets Council (who look after Trinity Square Gardens), the Severndroog Castle Campaign Group, the Revd Adrian Gatrill, RAF, Resident chaplain, St Clement Danes, the Battle of Britain Memorial Group and the SOE Memorial Group. Without the cooperation of these people and others too numerous to mention, the book would have been very difficult to complete. Lastly, I would like to thank my publishers who believed that my initial idea was achievable and have given us this opportunity to enjoy our wonderful city.

1

Richmond Park

Deer Me!

The famous residents of Richmond Park (© Giles Barnard)

The largest royal park, Richmond offers something for everyone throughout the year – from the famous deer, which you will see in several places as you walk, to kite-flying, bike hire, and even a view of St Paul's Cathedral. It is also a haven for wildlife, with several species of butterfly and birds, including kestrels and ring-necked parakeets to look out for. There are historical buildings, woods, ponds and plantations, and not far away is the River Thames as it bends itself away from the hustle and bustle of the city and out towards the western suburbs. We have started this walk at the Roehampton Gate car park, in the north-east 'corner' of the park, but you may find you wish to join the route at another point (see map) and leave the car at one of the other car parks around the periphery.

Getting there The Roehampton Gate car park (free at the time of writing) is reached from Upper Richmond Road West, the A205 (the South Circular). There are other car parks around the edge of the park. Alternatively, Richmond (District line), Barnes and Mortlake stations are all approximately 20–30 minutes' walk away from the north side of the park.
Length of walk 1 mile plus.
Time 2 hours plus.
Terrain Pathways and grass. Some of the paths are cycle ways so be careful when walking along with the children. Also remember that deer are wild animals so be careful when approaching a herd. Some inconsiderate people may let their dogs run free, which upsets the deer; they are perfectly safe to walk by as long as you don't frighten them.
Start Roehampton Gate car park.
Munch stop You will find plenty of places to picnic. There is a café at Roehampton Gate; also refreshment facilities at Broomfield Hill and Pen Pond car parks. Check the maps at the park for other food areas.

The Walk

1 Leave the car park and join the path in front of the café. Walk to the right. Cross the road at the entrance where you drove in and continue along, bearing to the left. Pass the sports fields on your left and divert on the right through Sheen Cross Wood.

Look out for different types of fungi through the wood, but do not touch.

Continue forward, running parallel with the road. Return to the main path when you reach the crossroads. Cross over the road towards the edge of the sports field, keeping it on your left, and take the pathway (no traffic) towards White Lodge.

2 Continue along this path, taking care not to upset any deer that are roaming freely in this area. Pass Duchess Wood on the right, and on the left you will see the amazing Georgian building of White Lodge.

I-SPY

If you listen carefully you may hear green ring-necked parakeets. Look up high in the trees opposite White Lodge and you may notice quite a number sitting together in the treetops.

***White Lodge** was originally a royal residence, built in 1727 as a hunting lodge for George II. It eventually passed, after many different owners, to Queen Victoria and Prince Albert. After further royal and private owners, in 1955 the Sadlers Wells Ballet School (now known as the Royal Ballet School) took it over and their students from age 11–16 are now in residence here.*

3 If you look down the next pathway on your right you will get a good view of Pen Ponds.

I-SPY

Keep a look out for more deer. See if you can spot a stag with its majestic antlers.

Walk forward along this path for a short way, keeping White Lodge on the left, and you will reach a car park that has a refreshment area; this appears to be open even during the winter months. Turn left at a small pathway alongside Spankers Hill Wood, going slightly uphill. There are benches here for a rest/munch stop. You can walk slightly forward and join the main path on your left if you prefer.

*Red and fallow deer were introduced by Charles I and can still be seen roaming freely. You must not feed them or approach them as they are wild but they are a great sight to see in their natural environment. **Richmond Park** is a National Nature Reserve and a Site of Special Scientific Interest. Please respect the wildlife that live here and, of course, do not leave litter.*

Beverley Brook

Pen Ponds are home to plenty of wildlife

4 Follow the path, keeping the wood to your left. Bear left, continuing along the pathway, alongside Treebox Wood, keeping the road on your right. Walk through some trees and the grassy areas of Victory Plantation. You will notice the area opening out. The path will veer slightly to the right and towards the bridge near Kill Cat Corner.

5 Cross the bridge and then go over the road, walking along the path with the road now on your left. There is a notice-board here with information on the wildlife you may have seen in the park. Continue back to the car park and café at Roehampton Gate.

You could extend the walk westwards to visit Pembroke Lodge but it would take around 30 minutes each way from Roehampton Gate car park. Alternatively, drive along Sawyers Hill and park at Pembroke Lodge car park.

1

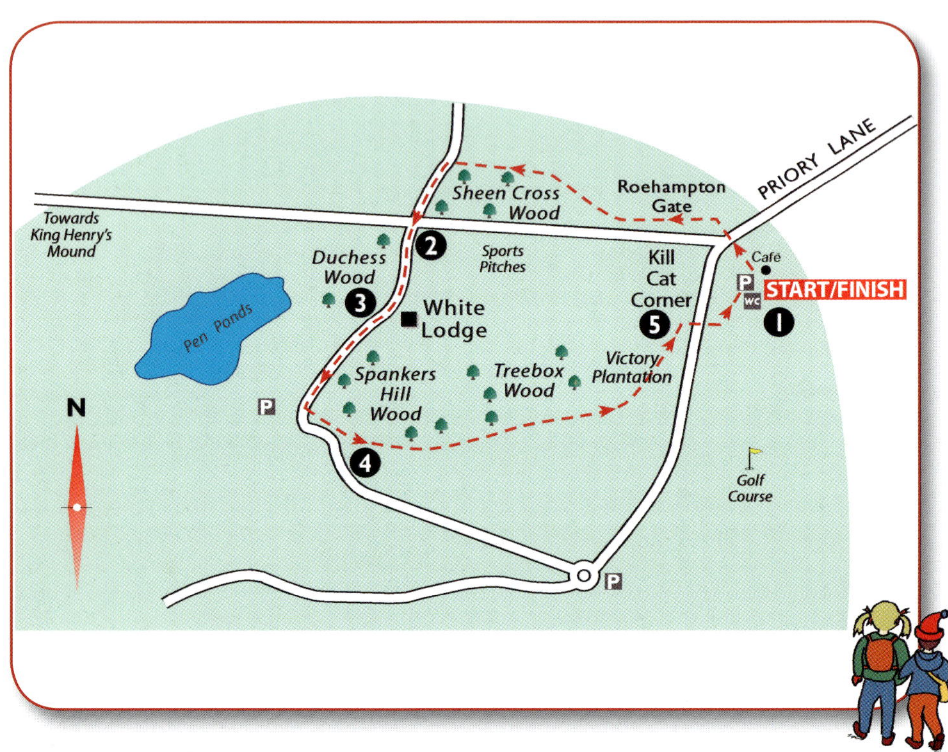

Pembroke Lodge *originally started life as a mole catcher's cottage; it was eventually extended into the building you see today. One of the residents was the former Prime Minister Lord John Russell, who lived there from 1847. It was also used during the Second World War for a secret intelligence group called the Phantom Squad. Today it is used as a conference centre and wedding venue but its grounds are open to the public and there is a café.*

The Ian Dury bench *at Poets Corner in the grounds of Pembroke Lodge commemorates the life of Ian Dury, a rock and roll singer during the 1970/1980s with a group called the Blockheads. The memorial bench is solar powered and enables people to plug in their headphones and listen to some of his songs.*

King Henry VIII's mound *is a wonderful viewpoint, with telescope, in the grounds of Pembroke Lodge. On a clear day you should be able to see St Paul's Cathedral to the east.*

2

Battersea Park

Tranquil Trekking

Kicking up the leaves

With **easy parking**, especially at the weekend, Battersea Park is a relaxing place to visit. It is situated alongside the River Thames and there is a great view across to the Royal Hospital, Chelsea. You may notice various sports taking place here, from Tai Chi in a quiet area, to cycling and jogging. Bikes can be hired in various shapes and forms and there is an adventure playground, so you might not be having just a restful stroll in this park if the children get their own way. The route passes Battersea Park Children's Zoo, so you could include a visit if you have time to spare.

2

Getting there Park at the north-east car park – turn off Queenstown Road, the A3216, onto Carriage Drive North. If arriving by public transport, you can access the southern area of the park from Battersea Park station which is on the BR line from Victoria and join the route in point 5 via Rosery Gate. One week to avoid for this walk is that of the Chelsea Flower Show at the end of May.

Length of walk 1 mile.

Time 2 hours plus.

Terrain Pathways and grass. Suitable for pushchairs/ wheelchairs.

Start The car park (pay and display) next to the Thames, off Carriage Drive North.

Munch stop You will find plenty of picnic areas in the park and a café overlooking the boating lake. There are toilets between the car park and the zoo on the left and also by the café in Carriage Drive North.

The Walk

Queen Victoria officially opened ***Battersea Park*** *in 1858. During the two world wars some of the area was used as allotments to provide much needed food. In 1951 parts of the park were turned into Pleasure Gardens with a funfair for the Festival of Britain. Every November the park holds a firework display and in July and August, a land train operates.*

1 From the car park, look across the river and you will see the Royal Hospital, Chelsea. Keeping the Thames on your right, join the main path. The toilets are here on the left. Walk past the zoo.

The Royal Hospital Chelsea*, a Sir Christopher Wren building, was completed in 1692 on land given by Charles II. As there was no place where sick and disabled soldiers could live it became their hospital. Nowadays it is known as the home for the Chelsea Pensioners. They are recognised by their bright red uniforms. The Chelsea Flower Show, which first started in 1913, is held annually in the grounds, transforming them into a floral masterpiece.*

Battersea Park Children's Zoo *is open all year round. For details visit the website www.batterseaparkzoo.co.uk or ☎ 020 7924 5826.*

2 Ahead you will see the Peace Pagoda on the right. Spend a little time walking around it.

I-SPY

Look to see how many gold Buddhas there are.

You may see a Buddhist monk tending to the area, so please treat it with respect – of course, no one is allowed to climb on it.

*Buddhist monks and nuns built the **Peace Pagoda** as part of the Peace Year in 1985. It is a place for all nationalities to visit in the hope that one day there will be peace across the world. A Japanese Buddhist monk, who relies on gifts of food, keeps the pagoda clean and tidy. An air of tranquillity surrounds it and you may see people meditating nearby.*

3 Continue along the main pathway of Carriage Drive North. Divert on your left through to the Grand Vista and Fountain Lake, which is on the right. Cross where the paths meet and continue walking across the sports pitches.

It is just to the right of here that Bastille Day celebrations take place in July. Visit www.wandsworth.gov.uk/ event office for further information.

4 Continue forward and the adventure playground is in front of you near to Sun Gate entrance. After a munch break and energy

The Peace Pagoda is a major landmark in the park

release, join the main path of Carriage Drive South. Follow the path east, passing the Sub-Tropical Gardens on your left. The gardens are a blaze of colour in the summer and during the winter months the plants are cocooned in a protective wrapping to keep them warm.

5 You will soon reach the lake.

I-SPY

Look out for herons, which can sometimes be seen nesting here in the early spring.

*Across the lake is the **Pump House.** This Victorian pumping station exhibits various artwork and also holds workshops and provides activities for children.*

Continue along and, as the pathway bends to the left just past Rosery Gate, you will reach the café.

6 After a well-earned rest continue along the pathway with the athletics track on your right. Pass the tennis courts and you will soon see the car park in front of you.

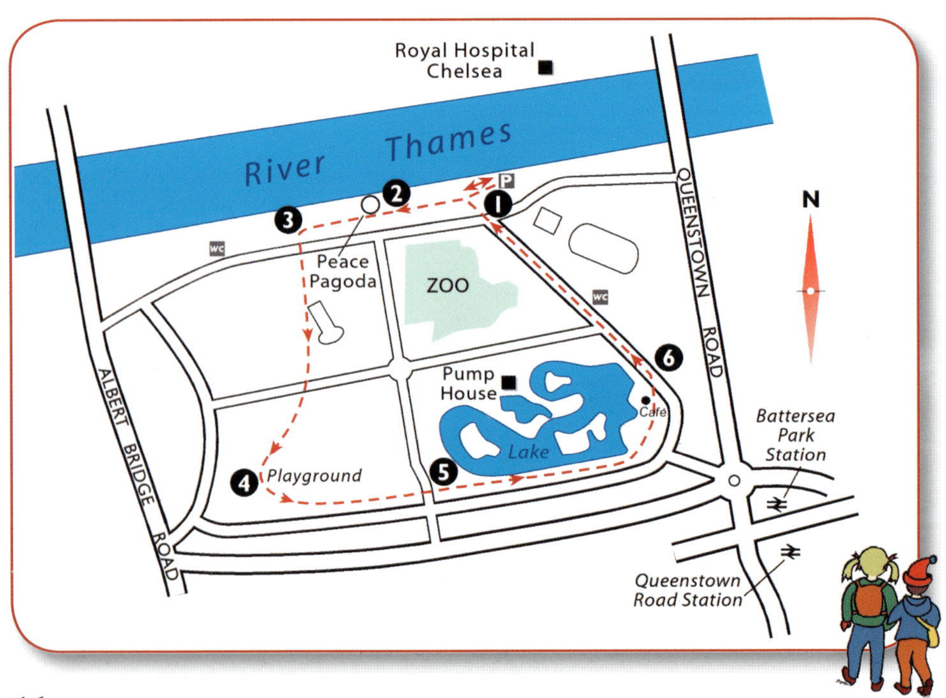

3

Kensington Gardens

The Princess and Peter Pan

Having fun in the Princess Diana Memorial Playground
(© Anne-Marie Briscombe)

Once part of neighbouring Hyde Park, Kensington Gardens has plenty to offer and is ideal for a family walk. Tributes to Queen Victoria and Prince Albert adorn this area and the route includes a short detour to the Albert Memorial, with the opportunity to marvel at the Royal Albert Hall. Diana, Princess of Wales lived in Kensington Palace and you follow part of her Memorial Walk. The feeling of childhood is all around as you pass Peter Pan's statue, remembering J.M. Barrie's stories of the Lost Boys. What with this and the fantastic playground, even the oldest of children can be transported back to Neverland – a truly magical experience.

3

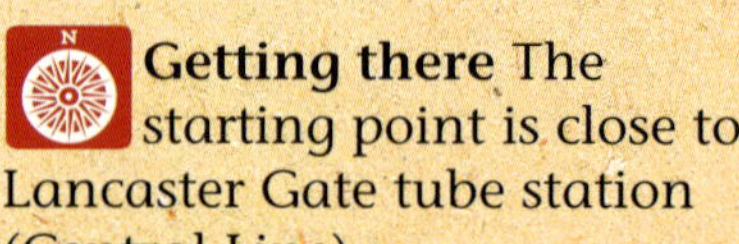

Getting there The starting point is close to Lancaster Gate tube station (Central Line).
Length of walk 1–2 miles although it can be shortened/lengthened depending on your route across the park. There are maps in the park marking out routes, along with very prominent signposts.
Time 2 hours plus.
Terrain Pathways. Suitable for pushchairs/wheelchairs throughout.
Start Marlborough Gate entrance, on the south side of Bayswater Road.
Munch stop The Lido Café in Hyde Park near to Serpentine Bridge (toilets alongside); also a café and toilets at the Memorial Playground. There are toilets at Marlborough Gate and near other entrances to the park.

The Walk

1 Enter at Marlborough Gate and walk south, keeping the fountains and the Long Water on your left. Follow the path towards Peter Pan's statue. You will find this slightly hidden on your right.

I-SPY

Look to see how many different birds you can spot on the lake.

Continue along the path and walk under West Carriage Drive into Hyde Park to see the Diana, Princess of Wales Memorial. If you continue a little further, you will come to the Lido Café and toilets. Spend some time paddling in the fountain, on your right, if the weather is hot enough. This is an ideal munch stop. Canada geese flock on the Serpentine and are a wonderful sight. You can also hire boats and pedalos nearby. This is where people swim over the festive period but it would be a bit too chilly for most.

The ***Peter Pan statue*** *is very ornate and it is well worth spending some time looking at the detail of the animals at the base. Set back slightly but overlooking the lake, Peter stands tall with a trumpet in his hand. There have been several films shot in this park, but the most relevant is* Finding Neverland, *based on the life of J.M. Barrie, the author of* Peter Pan. *Born in Scotland in 1860, he later lived near the park at 100 Bayswater Road, on the corner of Leinster Terrace. There is a blue plaque with his name outside this house. He would regularly visit Kensington Gardens whilst taking his dog for a walk and this was where*

Boating on the Serpentine (© Andy Lane)

he met the Llewellyn-Davies boys, who would be walking with their nanny. He based his stories of Peter Pan and the Lost Boys on these children. Before he died he left the copyright to his Peter Pan works to Great Ormond Street Hospital for Sick Children so they could benefit from any royalties paid. Outside the hospital entrance there are bronze statues of Peter Pan and Tinkerbell.

2 Retrace your steps and rejoin the path back into Kensington Gardens. Take the path towards the Serpentine Gallery and the Albert Memorial. Pass the gallery. Where the park opens out along the centre pathway, follow signs to the Albert Memorial. Divert left to reach the memorial and the large dome structure of the Royal Albert Hall at Queen's Gate.

The Peter Pan statue near the start of the walk

I-SPY

Look at the Albert Memorial and all the animals circling it. Can you see the camels? Take a moment to absorb the enormity of the Royal Albert Hall. See if you can see the frieze circling the top.

The ***Albert Memorial*** *was erected by Queen Victoria in memory of her husband, who died in 1861. After his death, she had all the railings in London painted black and she continued to wear black mourning clothes for the rest of her life. The animals surrounding the Albert Memorial represent the colonies: Africa, Asia, Europe and the Americas. Prince Albert's wish had always been to have a central building promoting the arts and sciences where the public could visit, so the Royal Albert Hall was built and officially opened in 1871. It holds many events. Due to its dome design, the sound generated within it is absolutely amazing. The*

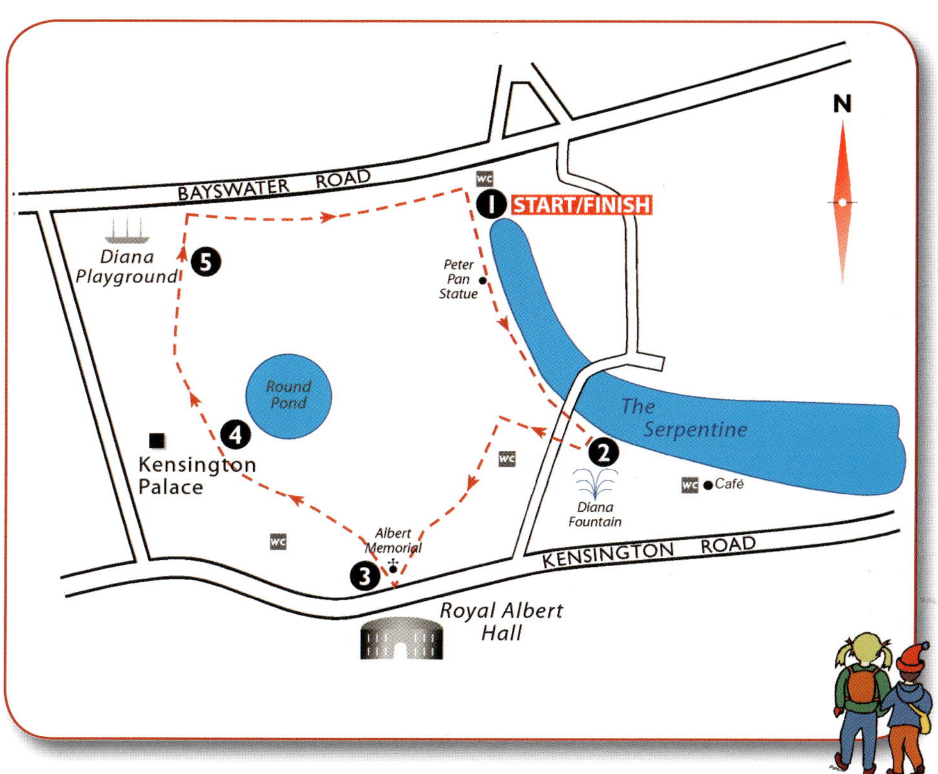

frieze around the outside is itself a masterpiece. Many famous people have appeared here, and choral festivals give even schoolchildren the opportunity to perform in this splendid hall. It also holds the yearly Poppy Service of Remembrance at which poppy petals fall, reminding us of all the people who have died in conflicts.

3 Leave the Albert Memorial and retrace your steps back to the path. Walk left and look for the signpost to the Diana Memorial Playground and Kensington Palace. You can cut through the trees here instead of following the main path. If you do, you will need to bear slightly right. Lots of sticks can be found here for an imaginary duel with Captain Hook. When you reach the main pathway of the Broad Walk, just near Kensington Palace, turn right and continue along, keeping the palace on your left and the Round Pond on the right. On Sunday

3

Standing to attention outside the Albert Hall

mornings, members of the Model Yacht Sailing Association sail their model craft on the pond.

***Kensington Palace** was where Queen Victoria was born in 1819. She lived here until she became Queen in 1837. Outside you will find a statue, which was sculptured by her daughter, Princess Louise, to celebrate 50 years of Victoria's reign. To date she is our longest serving monarch (20th June 1837 to 22nd January 1901).*

4 The statue of Queen Victoria is just in front of the palace.

I-SPY

Can you see the orb on the top?

Continue along the path, still following the sign for the playground. You come to the Elfin Oak on your left just outside the playground.

I-SPY

See if you can find the bird pulling out a worm.

On the right is the 'Time Flies' clock tower.

I-SPY

Look for the bird at the top.

Continue into the gated Diana, Princess of Wales Memorial Playground. Spend some time here having a picnic. Keep a look out for the crocodile. Be very worried if you hear a 'Tick, Tick, Tick'!

*The **Elfin Oak** is caged in order to protect it. A very old tree, it has been carved with various birds, animals and elves. Nearby is the 'Time Flies' clock tower and drinking fountain. Built in 1909, it is topped by a weather vane of a golden bird. The words 'Time Flies' are engraved under the clocks. For most of us this is only too true!*

***The Diana Memorial Playground**, opened in 2000, has been designed like a scene from Neverland. The large ship for the children to climb over sets the scene for meeting Captain Hook and you must be careful about any crocodiles you might find loitering nearby. Built as a memorial to the late Princess Diana, it is a wonderful tribute to a lady who loved children.*

5 After a well-earned play, rejoin the path and continue left along the Broad Walk. Turn right at the end, keeping the road to your left. Keep walking, either on the path or on the grass, towards the Marlborough Gate and Lancaster Gate station.

4

Regent's Park

Fit for a Prince

Enjoying a game of chase!

One of the royal parks, Regent's Park is situated in the centre of some very majestic buildings and during the summer is full of colourful blooms. The famous Open Air Theatre is within its Inner Circle. There is something for everyone and the park is a perfect place to spend a whole day. Within its grounds you will find London Zoo and you can look into some of the enclosures from the route of the walk, which also takes in the boating lake and various play areas and gives you access to the Regent's Canal and the sight of passing narrowboats at Primrose Hill Bridge. You may even get the opportunity to spot some celebrities as they walk their dogs or jog.

Getting there Underground: Great Portland Street (although you can access the park from other underground stations – Regent's Park, Baker Street, St John's Wood and Camden Town). Parking is available but it is wise to check the Royal Parks website for up-to-date information.
Length of walk 1 mile plus.
Time 2 hours plus.
Terrain Pathways. Wellies may be a good idea if you venture onto the grass, depending on the time of year. Suitable for pushchairs and wheelchairs.
Start The entrance to the park by Avenue Gardens, near to the Outer Circle and Park Square East.
Munch stop The park is perfect for picnics or there are various eating places/cafés.

The Walk

*Once part of the forest of Middlesex and belonging to the Abbesses of Barking, **Regent's Park** eventually became a royal hunting ground under Henry VIII. In 1811, the Prince Regent, later to become George IV, asked the royal architect, John Nash, to redesign the park so that it would be 'fit for a prince'.*

1 Take a stroll through Avenue Gardens and find the gargoyles supporting the Lion Tazza (from the Italian word for a cup) filled with flowers.

I-SPY

Can you count how many lions there are?

2 Walk down the main pathway, passing the Honest Sausage café, to the Ready Money Fountain, taking a diversion on the right towards Gloucester Gate. Here you will find children-only toilets and a very good playground. Near to the children's play area there is a rustic area with climbing frames made with wood and ropes.

*The **Ready Money Fountain**, which has been restored, is another public drinking fountain. It was a gift in 1869 from a very generous and kind Parsee man from Bombay, India, named Sir Cowasjee Jehangir, who later adopted the surname 'Readymoney'. It was a thank-you to the British people for the protection afforded to his people in India whilst the country was under British rule.*

3 Continue back to the fountain and walk ahead, taking the right-

4

The impressive Ready Money fountain

hand path alongside London Zoo. The zoo is on your right and you can get a view into some of the enclosures.

I-SPY

If you look carefully you may spot a camel or two on the right-hand side.

Pass the zoo and you will come to the turning to Primrose Hill Bridge over the Regent's Canal, on the right, where you can get a good view of passing narrowboats.

London Zoo opened *in 1827 and is the world's oldest scientific zoo. Housing over 700 species of animal,*

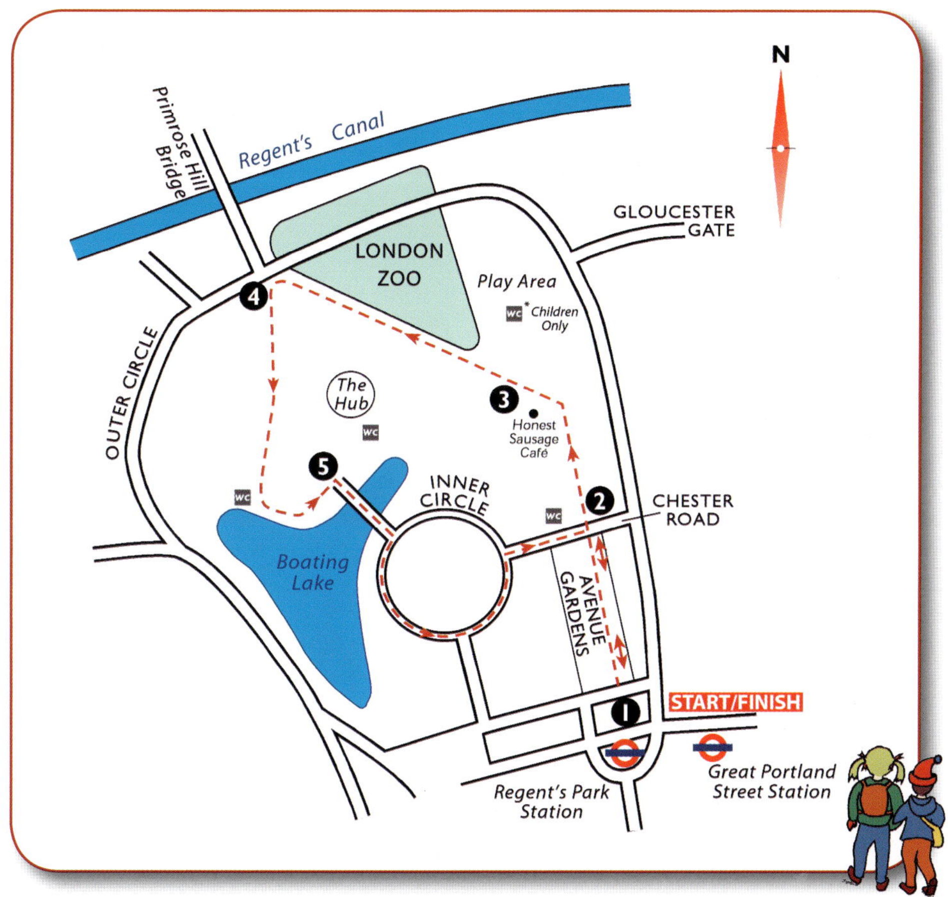

One of the many animals to be seen at the zoo

including amongst others, lions, tigers, camels, giraffes and monkeys, it also now boasts London's only living rainforest. It is open every day of the year except Christmas Day and details of admission prices can be found at www.zsl.org.

***See Walk 6** for more details about the canal. This is where the boats from Camden moor up to allow passengers to alight for a visit to London Zoo – or to take a boat back to Camden Market for a spot of shopping.*

4 Continue along the path, taking the second path on the left between the sports fields. Follow it along. Towards the end of this path is an ideal spot for a picnic and for the children to let off steam. You will find toilets on the right. In front you will see the boating lake.

Follow the path round to the left,

Scanning the canal for wildlife

keeping the lake on your right.

I-SPY

Look out for the different types of birds. How many species can you see?

5 Follow the path along and cross over the Longbridge on the right. Turn right along the Inner Circle. Continue walking along it, leaving by Chester Road. Turn right down Avenue Gardens and you are back at the start entrance. Just to the right of Avenue Gardens is a children's playground if they still have energy to burn. Signposts are frequent so it is easy to navigate.

5

Alexandra Palace

A View over London

Looking over the city at point 6 of the walk

Alexandra Palace was opened in 1873 and became known as 'The People's Palace' during the Victorian era – a place to relax and take in spectacular views of London. Now used as a conference centre and exhibition hall, its surrounding parkland can be enjoyed throughout the year and, with the changing seasons, there is something different to enjoy on each visit. If the weather is clear, you can get a great view of London even without the telescopes that are sited at the front of the building. The park is especially fun at the start of autumn when conkers are in abundance – watch out you don't get a bump on the head from one falling! There are two playgrounds for children of different age groups, also a skateboard park, together with a lake if you are feeling energetic and want to hire a boat or pedalo (this is seasonal so check before you come if you intend to do this) – altogether plenty to keep everyone amused.

Getting there This walk starts from the Grove car park, reached from the A504, Muswell Hill, via Alexandra Palace Way. However, there are car parks dotted all around the park grounds if you want to approach the route from a different direction. Alexandra Palace station is at the Wood Green entrance to the park with trains running from King's Cross, changing at Finsbury Park, or direct from Moorgate. The nearest underground station is Wood Green on the Piccadilly Line but it is a bus journey away.

Length of walk 2 miles plus, or you can shorten it by cutting across the park.

Time 2 hours plus if you stroll; more if you stop at the café or hire a boat.

Terrain Pathways but you will need sturdy shoes or wellies if the weather is inclement or you intend to divert from the paths. Suitable for pushchairs and wheelchairs.

Start The Grove car park (free parking) to the south-west of Alexandra Palace.

Munch stop There are a couple of cafés in the park and ample places to have a picnic so bring your blanket or, if you prefer, there are plenty of seats dotted about. Toilets can be found near the boating lake/café and the play area.

The Walk

1 Go through the car park and walk towards the Grove Café, which you will see on your right.

I-SPY

As you follow the path, look for some of the many different varieties of birds, such as robins, kestrels, song thrushes and finches.

Follow the path round to the left fork and keep your eyes peeled for the old oak tree, which is fenced off. There is a fallen tree nearby.

I-SPY

Can you count the rings and tell how old it is?

2 After diverting to the old oak, rejoin the path and continue walking forward. You will go through Lime Avenue, which was

How old is this tree?

a favourite haunt of Dr Samuel Johnson (compiler of the famous dictionary) in the 18th century, and walk towards the road. Passing the car park on the left and entrance to the garden centre on the right, cross the road, turn right and continue along the pathway. Walk down a short way and at the junction of two paths take the left one.

In the parkland, originally part of Tottenham Wood Farm, was once a large mansion called ***The Grove*** *and it was here that Dr Johnson used to visit his aristocratic friend, Sir Topham Beauclerk.*

3 At the fork in the path walk straight ahead. Turn right onto the tarmac path then turn left onto Lower Road, following the path leading to the helipad. On the right in the field you will see the 'H' marked out.

The helipad is used by famous people visiting events held at Alexandra Palace and the grass area next to the helipad was originally part of a racecourse in use from 1868 to 1970.

4 Continue along the path, keeping the field on your right, and take the path on the left at a clearing. Walk up the grassy field a short way and look for the half buried metal object. This is the barrage balloon weight.

The barrage balloon weight was used during the Second World War to tether the metal cables of the barrage balloons so that enemy aircraft would find it difficult to attack.

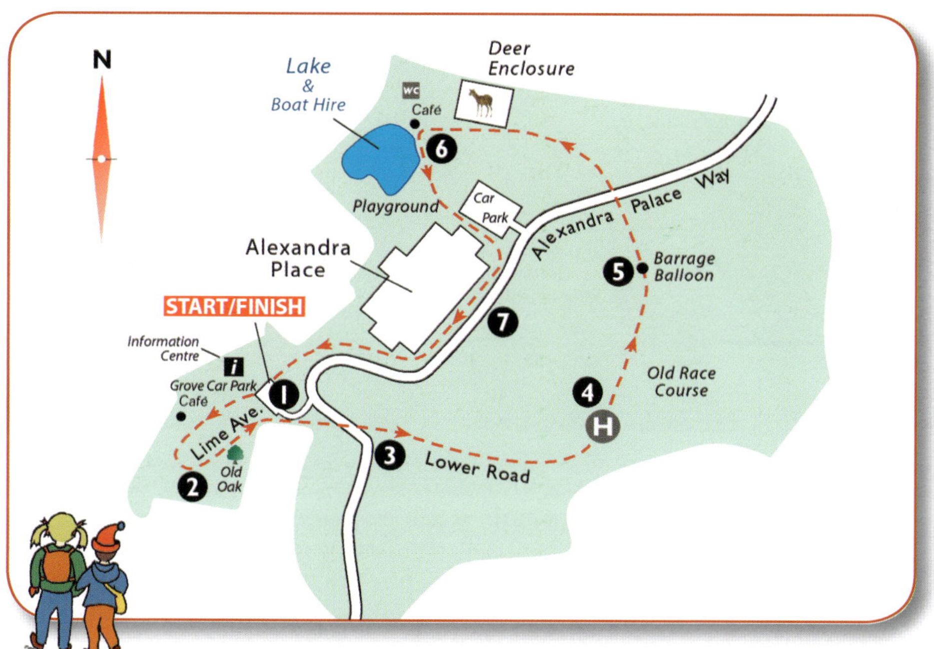

5

'Leo' outside the Grove café makes for a great photo opportunity

5 Continue walking up to join a smaller path and turn right along it, passing the pitch and putt area on your left. Be careful of stinging nettles and tufts of grass. (You can, if you prefer, walk back the way you have come, rejoin the path and continue until you reach the road ahead.) Continue straight on until you reach the

road. Cross over and turn left. Continue up the next path on your right, passing the stone marker and the ornate lamp. The deer enclosure is on the right. Follow the path up the hill and round. You will reach the café and boating lake on your right.

I-SPY

Keep a look out for a lion.

Even during the winter months, if the weather is dry it is very pleasant to sit outside the café and watch the wildlife. There are numerous birds to look out for especially on the boating lake, including coots – the black bird with the white head and beak – mallards, Canada geese and swans. Please be aware of the dangers of deep water and keep young children away from the edge.

A friendly squirrel

6 Leave the café area and, walking round the lake, you will see the children's play area in front. Resume the walk along the path, turning left out of the playground and round to the front of Alexandra Palace. This gives a fantastic view over London, especially on a clear day.

I-SPY

See if you can recognise any of the buildings. Then turn round and examine the front of the palace. Do you think it looks like the front of an old railway station? On the building you will notice a plaque marking the first transmission by the BBC in 1936.

There is a very informative website www.alexandrapalace.com and accommodating staff to answer any queries if you prefer to phone them ☎ (020 8883 3999).

7 Continue along the front of the palace, passing the restaurant at the side. Walk down to road level, joining the pavement at the main road, and return to the Grove car park on the right.

6

The Canal Museum to Camley Street Natural Park

Ice Cold and into the Countryside

Admiring the boats at Battlebridge Basin

Have you ever thought that ice could be shipped along the waterways of London and stored? Or even how the first ice cream came into being? The Canal Museum is small but very informative and although there is a small charge to enter, it is heaving with information. There are various displays and exhibitions on two floors, with Henrietta the Horse's trail for families along with a quiz sheet, answers for both of which can be found in the museum. On certain days during the holidays you can book to go on a riverboat trip into the Islington Tunnel and the price of the boat ticket includes admission to the museum. A small shop selling amongst other things, books, memorabilia and models is at the front. After spending a good hour or so here you can take a short walk, either beside the canal or along the road, to the nearby Camley Street Natural Park – one of the many gems hidden alongside the Regent's Canal. Here you can relax on a hot day overlooking the canal, pond dip with the children free of charge, learn about wildlife found around the area or hide in the living willow tepee.

Getting there Travel by main line or underground (Northern/Victoria/Circle/ Hammersmith & City/ Metropolitan) to King's Cross/St Pancras.
Length of walk 1 mile plus.
Time 1 hour plus in the museum, a short walk to Camley Street and any amount of time at the nature reserve – or you can do these walks on separate occasions.
Terrain Pavement but wellies may be needed in the reserve, depending on time of year. Suitable for pushchairs except by the canal path, which has some steps at the exit (unless you can carry the pushchair).
Start York Way, outside King's Cross/St Pancras.
Munch stop There is no café in the museum but they do sell ice cream in the summer months. There is room to eat a picnic at the reserve, and sandwiches, snacks and drinks are available at St Pancras station.

The Walk

1 From King's Cross turn left into York Way and then right into Wharfedale Road. Cross the road and take the second left into New Wharf Road. You will find the Canal Museum on your left.

From the outside one wouldn't realise there are enough treasures inside to keep your little 'treasures' amused, but this unassuming building gives a fantastic visual and practical insight into the history of the ice house and canal life generally. It was once an ice warehouse, built for Carlo Gatti

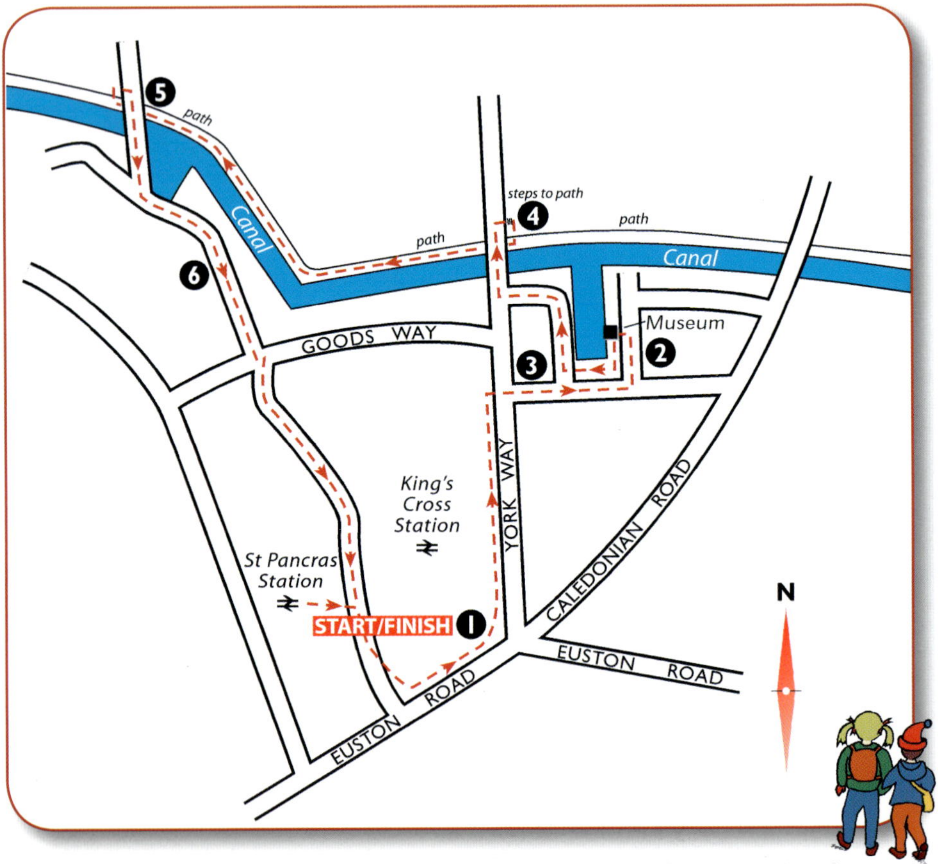

6

in approximately 1862 to store ice imported from Norway as the ice found in London wasn't as good. As refrigeration had not yet been invented it was difficult to make ice as easily as we can now. The first well had been dug in about 1857 and held a delivery of over 400 tons of ice.

The large ships would arrive in London at Limehouse Basin where the ice would be loaded onto barges led by horses. They would make their way along the Regent's Canal to **Battlebridge Basin**, where the ice would be unloaded into the deep wells and then sold to fishmongers, cafés and restaurants to keep their food fresh. Born in Switzerland in an area near to Italy and speaking Italian, Gatti had arrived in England *in 1847 and at first ran a stall selling sweet waffles. He wanted to start a business so decided to open a café and restaurant along with a fellow Swiss. At that time ice cream was expensive and only wealthy people able to afford such a luxury ever tasted it, but Gatti's innovative ice storage ideas meant that he could bring the taste of ice cream to the ordinary person. For details of opening times and the admission charge, see the website www.canalmuseum.org.uk or ☎ 020 7713 0836.*

2 As you commence your museum visit, you are greeted with a large, full-size narrowboat. Follow the Henrietta Museum Trail as it takes you on a trip into ice-cold history.

Step outside and see Battlebridge Basin. There are apartments built nearby but many people still permanently live on the canal boats.

I-SPY

Look at the paintings of canal roses on various items on the boats – at home, the children could try designing one of their own.

Return inside and look at the different types of bowls used to serve the ice cream.

I-SPY

Can you find the 'licking dishes'? Listen to the recording about Carlo Gatti and the ice trade. Look at the bicycle. Wouldn't it be fun if the ice cream man still made deliveries in this way? Before you venture to the next floor up, try and make the bridge in the play area. Upstairs take time to view the footage on the TV. It shows how the Regent's Canal played a very important part for London. Long before lorries came to our roads, the canals were a very busy place to be.

Leave the museum and turn right into New Wharf Road. At the end turn right again into Wharfedale Road and make another right turn into Crinan Street, which cuts off the corner.

3 Continue along and you will come out into York Way. Walk to the right over the bridge and then on your right you follow the slope going down towards the canal path.

*The **Regent's Canal** was opened between 1816 and 1820 and named after the Prince Regent. Originally barges were horse-drawn and the boatman would use a gauging rod to measure the depth of the boat in the water. This told him how heavy the cargo was that he had on board.*

6

The horses were well looked after as without them it would have been very difficult to pull the barges along the canals. There are many locks along the Regent's Canal. One is along the canal path near to the nature reserve. If you get the opportunity, it is interesting to watch how the boats pass through the lock gates. It can be quite time consuming waiting for the lock to fill up to the level where the boat can pass through without dropping a great height. You may also see wildlife along the canal and even people fishing. The Regent's Canal flows through Camden, passing London Zoo (see Walk 4) and joining the Thames in the east. You can book boat trips from Camden Lock along the canal, taking in the sights from another angle.

4 Turn right once you reach the canal. Watch out for cyclists, as this is a very busy stretch of pathway. Go under the tunnel.

I-SPY

Here you will find large indentations made by ropes on the tunnel walls. Look out for people fishing. You may even be fortunate to see a swan or two on the other side of the riverbank.

As you proceed along you will eventually come to a lock gate.

I-SPY

As the canal is usually busy with boating traffic, there may even be a boat navigating the lock as you pass by.

5 Just a little way along you will come to some steps that lead you back onto the road above at the Camley Street bridge. Exit here and turn right along Camley Street. Carefully cross the road at the junction of Granary Street and follow the road under the railway bridge. Cross over and the nature reserve entrance is on your left.

Originally used as a coal yard, the nature reserve was created in 1984. It is open every day throughout the year. For more details, visit the website www.wildlondon.org.uk or ☎ 0207 833 2311.

6 Walk to the left of the visitor centre and make your way along the side of the canal. There is a bench here and you can get a good view of the activity on the canal. The reserve isn't so big that you will be tired out but it is a peaceful place in which to sit and relax. Find time to explore and hunt for bugs and butterflies. Pick up your pond dipping equipment from the visitor centre along with any instructions from the helpful staff, if you haven't been pond dipping before.

Follow the pathway to the pond.

Please be careful near the water and do not let children pond dip without an adult present. Lying on tummies to put in the net is the recommended technique. After you have found what lives beneath and if it is summertime, you have most probably been teased by a dragonfly, finish your walk.

Return to the entrance and turn left.

Although now modernised and incorporating the Eurostar to the Continent, ***St Pancras*** *still retains its Victorian charm. Inside the station there are two bronze statues, one of a couple in an embrace and another of Sir John Betjeman, the poet, who saved the station from demolition in the 1960s.*

Enjoying a spot of pond dipping in the nature reserve

7

Charing Cross to Buckingham Palace via St James's Park

A Romp to the Palace

Changing of the Guard at Buckingham Palace

This is a wonderful route for children, taking you past some of London's most famous landmarks, including Trafalgar Square, Cleopatra's Needle, The Mall, Buckingham Palace and Horse Guards Parade, giving the whole family a lot to look at. There is plenty of safe space for a run about in St James's Park, and some marvellous trees for games of hide and seek. If you are doing the walk in the morning (and on a day when it is taking place), don't miss the ceremony of the Changing of the Guard in front of the palace – see details below.

Getting there Make your way to Villiers Street at the entrance to Charing Cross underground station (Bakerloo and Northern line).
Length of walk 2 mile round trip including walking to the front of Buckingham Palace.
Time 1 hour plus, but you can spend any length of time in the park (and add time for Changing of the Guard).
Terrain Mostly pavements. Suitable for pushchairs. Wellies might be needed in the park, depending on the time of year.
Start Villiers Street, outside Charing Cross tube station.
Munch stop There are various cafés and supermarkets on the route and the Inn the Park restaurant and refreshment vans in St James's Park (not to mention good picnic spots in the park). Toilets are available along the Embankment (just opposite Cleopatra's Needle) offering free baby changing facilities; a charge is payable for the toilet but there is an attendant. Toilets in the park can be located by the easy to read map situated near to the park entrance at the Artillery Memorial (point 5).

The Walk

1 Starting at Charing Cross station, turn right into Villiers Street. This takes you downhill past restaurants, cafés and shops. Just before you reach the bottom of the street on the left-hand side you will pass a house where Rudyard Kipling, the author of *The Jungle Book*, lived from 1889 to 1891. Continue towards the river and turn left into Victoria Embankment Gardens.

2 As you enter the gardens you will see Buckingham Watergate on the left – this was the original gateway to the Thames at this point before the shape of the river was altered and the Embankment built in the 1860s. Continue walking through the gardens towards the river.

7

I-SPY

Look up and down the Thames and notice the different types of boats. Are they all carrying passengers? Can you see the River Police patrolling the river?

It is hard to believe that hundreds of years ago the river was busier than some of the streets. The Thames was used not only to bring in goods from overseas but also to ferry wood and stone to rebuild the city after the Great Fire of London. A 'waterman' would row passengers across the river; they were trained boys and men who were like boat taxi drivers. A 'lighterman' would be in charge of cargo boats. In the winter of 1814, it was so cold that the river froze over though nowadays the river is too fast flowing for it to freeze completely.

3 On reaching the main road, turn right onto the Embankment. Cross the road.

I-SPY

Here you will see Cleopatra's Needle. Take a look at the benches nearby. Can you find some small sphinxes? You get a very good view of the London Eye from here.

Cross back and turn into Northumberland Avenue. At the end of this road there are some arches in front of the shops.

I-SPY

If you look carefully you can see different animals carved into the stone. Try and recognise ten different animals. Have you spotted the car with the sea creatures?

Cleopatra's Needle *has an amazing history. Over 3,500 years old, this stone obelisk was originally erected by the ancient Egyptians in the city of Heliopolis, which is near Cairo. When the Romans came they moved the obelisk to the port of Alexandria as a kind of trophy. After the Romans had left it was knocked down and lay buried in the sand for almost 2,000 years. It was brought to London in 1878 and nearly sank with its ship on the voyage over. The needle has nothing to do with Queen Cleopatra, as it was already over 1,000 years old when she was Queen of Egypt, but it came from her city. At a height of 68 ft and weighing 180 tons, there is a Victorian time capsule buried beneath which is said to include: a newspaper, a set of coins, a razor, four bibles in different languages and, we are told, photos of 12 of the most beautiful women of that time!*

A classic view of the Thames

The ***London Eye*** *was opened in 2000 as a monument for the new Millennium. Its 32 pods, one for each London Borough, give great views over London. It can also be seen from St James's Park and looks fantastic lit up after dark. Standing 443 ft high, it goes round at 0.6 miles per hour, slowly enough for people to step on and off without it stopping.*

4 You have now reached Trafalgar Square and Nelson's Column. Take the second left, carefully crossing the road into The Mall. Follow this through Admiralty Arch. The statue on your left is of Captain James Cook, the first English explorer to reach Australia. Just after the Police Memorial on the left you

reach a colourful map detailing the area and its interesting features. You can either continue walking down The Mall towards Buckingham Palace or walk through the park.

I-SPY

If you walk along The Mall (NB: on Sundays it is usually closed to traffic) look up at the original lampposts. Can you see the ships on top? They are replicas of the ships in Admiral Nelson's fleet – the array is known as 'Nelson's Fleet that never sailed'.

***Trafalgar Square** has been a great London meeting place for people over the decades. You can see Vice-Admiral Horatio Nelson standing proudly on his column. His statue was put up to commemorate the Battle of Trafalgar in 1805 and it is over 150 ft high – that's twice the height of Cleopatra's Needle. The statue of Charles I on horseback was the site of the original Charing Cross. A Christmas tree, sent by the Norwegians as a 'thank you' for British help during the Second World War, is erected here every December and on New Year's Eve huge crowds gather to see in the New Year.*

*As you pass through Admiralty Arch it is worth looking out for the **'London Nose'**, a small stone nose poking out from the wall in the right-hand archway. Children will need to be lifted to see it, as the height was suited to men on horseback (you must watch out for the traffic coming towards Trafalgar Square). It is said to have been good luck for the soldiers to touch before they went into battle.*

5 As you enter the park take the right-hand fork. This leads you through the trees – an ideal spot for a picnic. The enormous trees are great for playing hide and seek.

Follow the path along and you come to a crossroads. Venture straight on towards the lake.

I-SPY

Here on the left you should be able to see pelicans. If you go near to the water there is an information board detailing the species of wildfowl in the park. Black swans can be seen here along with the more traditional kind. Pelicans may also be seen from Duck Island (point 7), where they are fed every day between 2.30pm and 3pm.

Continue along the path with the lake on your left.

Horatio Nelson stands atop his column in Trafalgar Square

6 At the far end, leave the park and join The Mall on the right. You will find yourself in front of the Queen Victoria Memorial. Walk carefully past, watching out for any traffic, and you are in front of Buckingham Palace.

I-SPY

Do you remember the song about 'Changing Guards at Buckingham Palace'? You may see the guards changing their posts. Do they have different uniforms? Take a few photos and have a quick glance to see if the Queen is at home (this is usually when the Royal Standard flag is flying).

Proceed back the way you came through the park. Walk back to the bridge and cross over. If you pause for a moment, you can get great views from the bridge.

***Buckingham Palace** opens its doors during the summer months to visitors. You are able to visit the Queen's Gallery, displaying items from the royal collection such as furniture and paintings. The Palace has 775 rooms of which 52 are bedrooms and 78 are bathrooms. The Queen and Prince Philip are not the only members of the royal family to live there. It also includes the London residences of the Duke of York, and the Earl and Countess of Wessex and their children. During the summer, the Royal Garden Parties take place, when tea, sandwiches and cakes are served in large marquees. To get an invitation you have to be nominated by someone from a charity or organisation.*

*The Guards outside the palace are working soldiers of the Household Division. They are made up of the Household Cavalry, the Life Guards, Blues and Royals and five other regiments of foot guards. The Household Cavalry are on horseback and the foot guards wear the bearskins and red tunics. The **Changing of the Guard ceremony** takes place daily during the summer months, usually at 11.30 am (get there at least 15 minutes early – but many people arrive long before that). In the winter months it is usually on alternate days. Make sure you check the Changing of the Guard website (www.changing-the-guard.com) before you set out if you want to include this with your walk.*

7 Continue back along the other side of the lake, passing Duck Island. Walk to the edge of the park and cross Horse Guards Road. Turn left and enter Horse Guards Parade on your right.

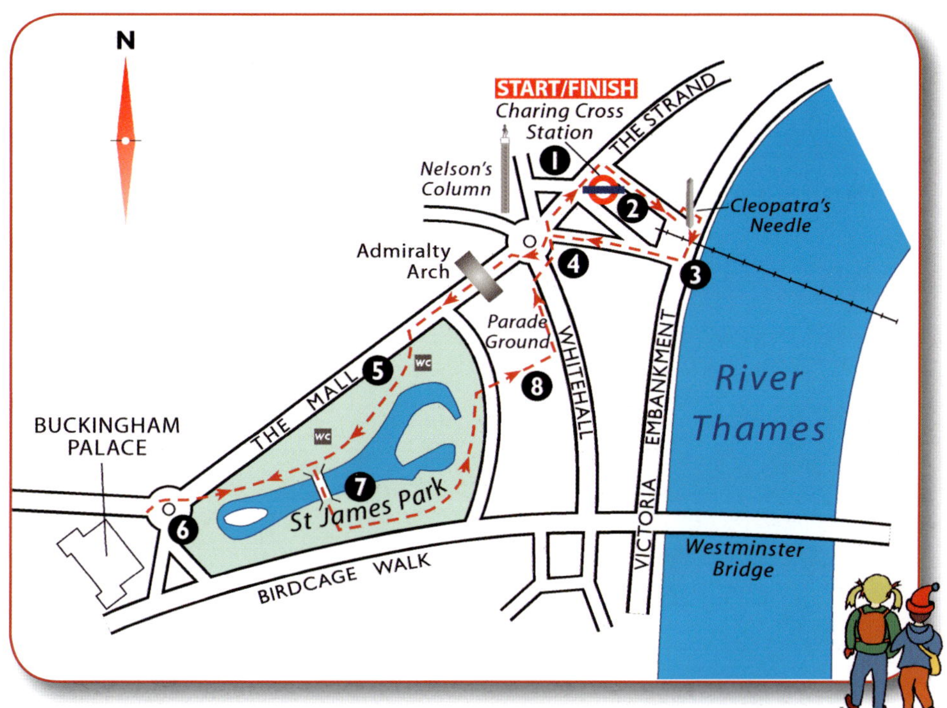

Stroll across the parade ground and pass through the walkway next to the Household Cavalry Museum and into the courtyard.

There is a small shop to buy London novelties on the right and photo opportunities with the guards, but don't make them laugh! Proceed through the arch.

I-SPY

You may see the mounted horses here who are on parade between 10 am and 4 pm each day.

8 Turn left into Whitehall, cross the road and continue until you reach Trafalgar Square with its fountain in the centre and guarding lions. Cross over Northumberland Avenue and take the next right into the Strand. Charing Cross station is a short way up on your right.

8

Westminster from Both Sides of the River

Famous People

Posing for the classic 'tourist' shot on a bright sunny day.

There are plenty of statues of famous people for the children to see along this route, which starts near the splendid bronze figure of Winston Churchill at Westminster, crosses Lambeth Bridge, goes back over the river at Hungerford Bridge and finishes alongside Boudicca in her chariot. Seeing Big Ben and the Houses of Parliament up close is always exciting and, on the other side of the river, you can gaze up at the towering pods of the London Eye. This very enjoyable circular stroll includes stretches of the Jubilee Walk on both sides of the Thames.

Getting there Westminster underground station is on the Circle, District and Jubilee lines.
Length of walk 1 mile approx.
Time 2 hours (more if you want to visit the Florence Nightingale Museum).
Terrain Pavements and a few steps.
Start Outside Westminster tube station.
Munch stop Victoria Tower Gardens and Jubilee Gardens are good picnic places. There are also fast food outlets and toilets near the Dali Museum and the London Aquarium, with food also available close to the London Eye.

The Walk

1 Come out of Westminster station and walk towards Parliament Square, keeping the Houses of Parliament on your left. You will be able to see Winston Churchill's statue and on your left is Big Ben. Continue into Margaret Street, keeping on the same side as the Houses of Parliament. Look for the statue of Oliver Cromwell outside. Continue along the pavement and look to the left outside St Stephen's entrance.

Can you see the crowned lions?

Continue forward into Old Palace Yard. On the right is Westminster Abbey. Continue along, approaching the Sovereign's Entrance. Who do you think may use this entrance?

***Winston Churchill** was a Member of Parliament and later became Prime Minister for five years during the Second World War, and then again for four years in the 1950s. His famous speeches are still quoted today.*

*The **Houses of Parliament**, also known as the Palace of Westminster, are made up of the House of Lords and the House of Commons. This is where the Prime Minister and all the politicians meet. At the State Opening of Parliament in November, the Queen attends, arriving in the State Coach, wearing the crown that is stored at the Tower of London. Up until 1512 the Palace of Westminster was home to kings and queens. Big Ben – or rather St Stephen's Tower (which is actually the clock tower) – is part of the Palace of Westminster. Big Ben is, in fact, the 13-tonne bell itself, with its very familiar striking sound.*

8

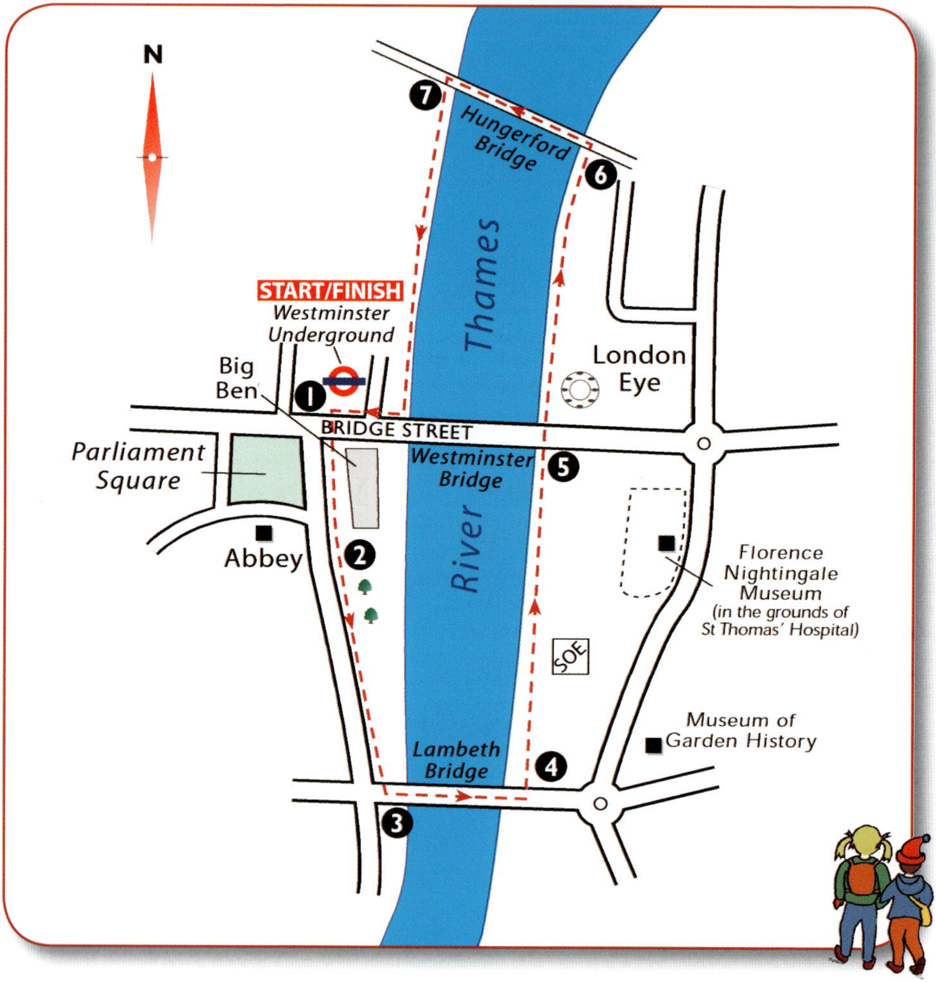

2 As the road continues into Abingdon Street, turn left into Victoria Tower Gardens. This is an ideal spot for a picnic and run about in the shadow of the House of Lords. There are plenty of seats available and you can, if you wish, overlook the Thames. After a well-earned break, walk through the park following the 1977 Jubilee Walk, keeping the Thames on your left. When you reach the end, walk up the steps and onto Lambeth Bridge.

I-SPY

Look out for the pineapples on the bridge.

*The **Jubilee Walk** was created in 1977 to celebrate Queen Elizabeth II's Silver Jubilee. As you walk along, you will notice large round plaques at every junction. If you look carefully at the crown on each of the plaques, you will see that the cross on it points in the direction of the walk.*

3 Follow the Jubilee Walkway over Lambeth Bridge, stopping to have a look along the Thames and wave to the passing boats. Go down the steps on the other side, keeping the Thames on your left.

*As you walk back down the riverside walkway, the building to your right is the **Garden Museum** (formerly known as the Museum of Garden History), which is housed in the former St Mary at Lambeth church, alongside Lambeth Palace, home to the Archbishop of Canterbury. As you pass the benches can you see the swan head? Look up at the lampposts: these have black-painted fish and a small crown on the top.*

Violette Szabo

On the right, notice the stone head of a lady, Violette Szabo. This is the memorial to the SOE (Special Operations Executive). Just along from this is a small drinking fountain.

4 Continue along the Jubilee Walk.

I-SPY

You will be able to take a great photo of the Houses of Parliament and Big Ben.

On the right is the back of St Thomas' Hospital.

*The **Special Operations Executive** was a group of secret agents set up during the Second World War. It is only in recent years, due to information regulations being lifted, that we are able to commemorate the brave people who were part of this team. Some were women who were dropped by parachute* *into occupied France; they assisted with breaking codes and sending information back to Britain or helped with the resistance groups. Some were captured and tortured and their final resting place is the country in which they landed. Violette Szabo was one of those agents. She originated from Brixton, daughter of a French mother and English father. Although she never made it back to Britain, she was one of the bravest secret agents we had. Even while she was being tortured she never gave any information away. She was only 23 years old when she died.*

5 The next bridge is Westminster. Here you can divert to the Florence Nightingale Museum; there are signs showing the way. Continue the walk along the riverbank and under the tunnel, coming out by the Movieum of London, which exhibits various memorabilia and props from well-known films. You will find plenty of places to eat along here on your right. Next is the London Aquarium.

I-SPY

Can you see the long-legged elephant sculpture and spot the insects on the sculpture outside the Dali Universe museum?

The London Eye is in front of you and the Jubilee Gardens are on your right. This is another place for a picnic as well as having a choice of refreshment outlets. You may also see street performers.

*Also known as 'the Lady with the Lamp', **Florence Nightingale** set up a field hospital during the Crimean War in Turkey (1853–1856), helping wounded soldiers. She later founded a training school for nurses at St Thomas' Hospital where there is now a museum dedicated to her life. The website www.florence-nightingale.co.uk will give you more details.*

*For details of the **London Eye** see Walk 7.*

6 After a well-earned rest, continue along beside the river and walk up the steps to Hungerford Bridge. There is a lift if required.

I-SPY

Look at the map on the bridge showing London landmarks and where they are positioned in relation to where you are standing.

7 Once across the bridge, walk down to road level and turn towards the river (keeping it on your left). Continue walking along the Victoria Embankment.

Part of the Battle of Britain Memorial

Here you will see boats that are permanently moored. Have a close look at the Battle of Britain Memorial on the right.

I-SPY

Can you make out the aeroplanes and children hiding from the bombing? What famous landmarks can you see on the memorial?

Continue along and look up to the right at a large statue of Boudicca in her chariot. Big Ben is right in front of you. You are now back at Westminster station.

*The **Battle of Britain Memorial** on the Embankment was unveiled on the 65th anniversary in 2005. A detailed memorial depicting various scenes from the Battle of Britain, it commemorates the airmen who took*

Boudicca and her chariot

part. Engraved below it is a famous quotation from Winston Churchill. More information can be found at www.bbm.org.uk

***Boudicca** was a Celtic queen of the Iceni tribe who ruled East Anglia during Roman times. She led her army into London to overthrow the Romans around AD 61. Boudicca was eventually captured with her daughters and they took poison rather than live under Roman rule. Her powerful statue, in the shadow of Big Ben completed in 1905, sees her standing in her chariot with her daughters.*

9

Lincoln's Inn Fields and Covent Garden

Fruit 'n' Flowers

Watching the entertainment in Covent Garden

We start this walk by strolling through Lincoln's Inn Fields – sometimes you might be lucky enough to see film crews and it is worth asking them what they are filming as you may be able to watch it in the future on television or at the cinema. On this fascinating circuit we pass what may be the oldest shop in London, have a look at St Clement Danes church, which seems to be in the middle of the road, and experience the hustle and bustle of the market at Covent Garden. This is now full of craftsmen selling all sorts of gifts and it is hard to believe that it was once a thriving fruit, vegetable and flower market. It is well worth watching the street entertainers in the piazza and, when you walk through the Apple Market, there are others keeping the crowds amused at the opposite end of the building. We complete the route by entering the heart of Theatreland.

Getting there Holborn station is on the Central and Piccadilly lines.
Length of walk Approximately 1–2 miles.
Time 1 hour plus walking, but you can spend any length of time in Lincoln's Inn Fields and Covent Garden.
Terrain Pavement. Suitable for pushchairs and wheelchairs.
Start Outside Holborn station, in Kingsway.
Munch stop Lincoln's Inn Fields are a good place for a picnic. There are various cafés en route and small supermarkets are dotted about. Toilets are available in Lincoln's Inn Fields, behind the church of St Clement Danes and also at Covent Garden next to St Paul's church.

The Walk

1 From Holborn station turn left into Kingsway. Walk along and take a left into Remnant Street. Lincoln's Inn Fields are in front of you. Enter the park through the gates. The pathway outside follows the perimeter of the park but if you are hungry it is a pleasant place to picnic while the children play. In the centre is a bandstand. When you have finished your munch stop exit at the corner nearest the tennis courts.

*Despite appearing quite a peaceful place now, **Lincoln's Inn Fields**, the largest public square in London, was once a place that held horrific events. The plaque on the floor of the pavilion explains that it was the site where William, Lord Russell was beheaded for plotting to assassinate Charles II. Nowadays it is more peaceful. On the outside perimeter of the park you will find the Hunterian*

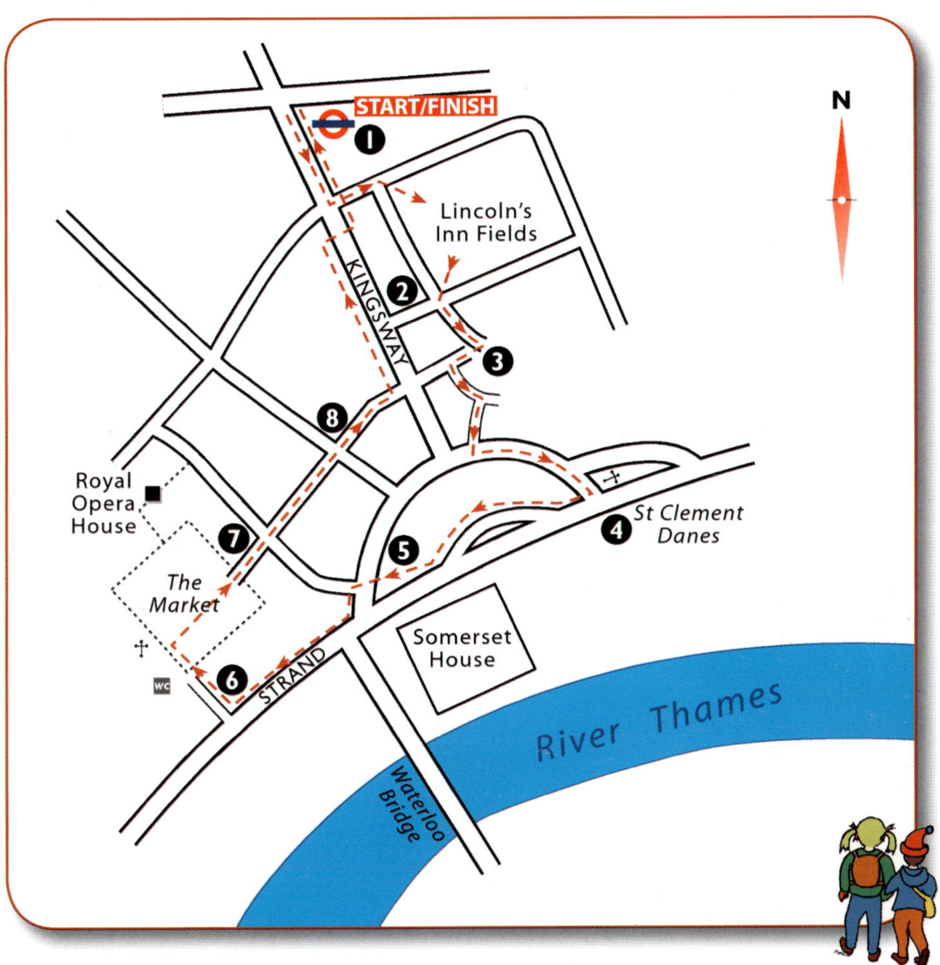

Museum (free entry), which exhibits various medical instruments and, on the other side, the Sir John Soane's Museum (free entry), which displays his various collections.

2 Cross the road and turn left into Portsmouth Street. On the left you will see the Old Curiosity Shop, built in 1567 and possibly the oldest shop in London, crooked and very out of place in between modern buildings. The painted notice on the front says that it was 'immortalised by Charles Dickens'.

9

I-SPY

Close your eyes for a moment and imagine you can hear the clip-clopping of hooves on the cobbled streets.

Bringing you back to the present, cross the road.

I-SPY

See if you can spot the date on the floor outside the George IV pub.

Throughout the City and West End of London you will find many places associated with ***Charles Dickens****, the famous writer of* Oliver Twist, Nicholas Nickleby *and* A Christmas Carol, *to name just a few of his books. Dickens lived not too far away, in Doughty Street, now the Dickens Museum. Living and working in London he made observations and based his stories on real-life events and people who were about at the time. The Old Curiosity Shop with its small windows helps us to imagine what it would have been like in the time of Oliver Twist.*

3 Turn right into Portugal Street and left into Clare Market.

I-SPY

Have you noticed any elephants in the area by the name of Baby Tembo?

Turn right into Houghton Street and left into Aldwych. Cross the road very carefully and you reach the church of St Clement Danes (otherwise known as the RAF church) in the centre of the road.

***Baby Tembo* is** *a bronze sculpture, placed near the London School of Economics in 2002 as a gift from a Mr and Mrs Odette of Toronto whose son attended the LSE.*

Baby Tembo

The well-known nursery rhyme 'Oranges and lemons, say the bells of St Clements' was thought to be based on the bells ringing at the church of ***St Clement Danes****. The second church to be built on this site was by Sir Christopher Wren. During the Second World War it was bombed very badly but it was rebuilt in 1958. Look on*

The statue of Dr Samuel Johnson at the rear of St Clement Danes church

the wall near to the door and you will notice the RAF wings. On the wall behind the statue of Dr Johnson, you can see the shrapnel marks made by the falling bombs during the war.

4 With your back to the church, cross the road in front of the statue of Gladstone and walk towards Australia House. Glance across to the original entrance to Strand station on the Piccadilly line. Continue walking alongside Australia House and pass the entrance where Gringotts Bank was filmed for the *Harry Potter* films. The next building you come to is the BBC's Bush House.

I-SPY

Can you see the large lion doorknockers?

William Ewart Gladstone *was Prime Minister four times during the Victorian Age and died in 1898. He is buried at Westminster Abbey.*

5 Look across the road and you will see a grand entrance to Somerset House. If you have time, cross the Strand and venture inside. There is a café here, along with the Courtauld Gallery (free admission to the gallery for children). Walk through to look at the fountains and the statues.

I-SPY

Don't miss Old Father Thames.

Retrace your steps and cross back again.

I-SPY

Look at the building on the corner of Wellington Street. Ship ahoy!

Continue along the Strand. Look to the other side of the road and you will see Savoy Court and the Savoy Hotel.

Somerset House *sits quietly along the Strand. The archway opens into a large area that reaches down to the river. As you enter from the Strand and walk through, Old Father Thames sits proudly ready to greet visitors. During the summer months you can picnic in the grounds and if the fountains are working, many dip their toes in the cool water. During certain winter months the courtyard is turned into a spectacular ice rink.*

Back along the Strand, hidden down a small turning called Savoy Court you will find the ***Savoy Hotel****. The* ***Savoy Palace*** *was originally built here and nearby is the* ***Savoy Theatre****, the first to be lit by electricity. Wat Tyler and his accomplices burnt the palace to the ground during the Peasants' Revolt in 1381; the poor people in medieval times wanted to be treated fairly and so they stood up to the richer people by protesting. The Savoy Hotel has seen many famous guests including the Beatles and Claude Monet, who painted the view from his room overlooking the River Thames. Savoy Court is the only street in the United Kingdom where all vehicles have to drive on the right.*

6 Turn right into Southampton Street, walking slightly uphill. Facing you will be Covent Garden. Jubilee Market is on your right

and well worth a visit. Continue into the Covent Garden piazza in front of you.

I-SPY

Here you can watch the entertainers. Don't get too close to the front otherwise they might entice you to join in!

On the left of the piazza is St Paul's church, otherwise known as 'The Actors' Church' with a small garden with seating and also toilets. There is a plaque explaining that the first Punch's Puppet Show in England was performed on this spot and witnessed by Samuel Pepys in 1662.

7 Leave Covent Garden through the Apple Market and continue forward into Russell Street. You have entered Theatreland. When you reach Bow Street cross over and look down towards your left. The white building you can see with the pillars is the Royal Opera House.

I-SPY

Look for the theatre masks and the instruments on the pillars.

On the right of the street is the Theatre Royal Drury Lane. To the left of the entrance is a large drinking fountain. Walking alongside the building you pass the stage door.

I-SPY

Watch out for actors going in and out.

***Theatre Royal Drury Lane** is one of the most famous theatres in Theatreland. First built in the reign of James I then rebuilt by Sir Christopher Wren, the building you see now opened in 1812. Seating 2,205 people, it has shown many of the largest productions in the West End.*

8 At the end of the road, cross over and stop at the front of an unusual restaurant, called Sarastro. If the doors are open, peer inside.

Continue along the side into Kemble Street underneath the flower arches. Turn left at the end into Kingsway. Cross the road at the crossing and continue along until you reach Holborn station.

***Sarastro** can't be missed! During the summer months colourful flowers are in abundance. Inside it has theatre boxes where people sit to eat their meals whilst being entertained by operatic performers.*

10

The Monument and the Museum of London

London's Burning

The London Stone – perhaps the city's oldest landmark

This interesting walk will help to bring one of the main topics of London history – the Great Fire of 1666 – alive for children. The route starts at the Monument, the height of which reflects its distance from the start of the fire, passes the Golden Boy statue at

Pye Corner, where the fire is thought to have ended, and finishes at the Museum of London with its fascinating 'War, Plague & Fire' gallery. On the way you will also see the London Stone, wander through Paternoster Square to get close to St Paul's Cathedral, pass the former Newgate Prison and encounter Henry VIII at St Bart's – with the buildings of various livery companies to look at as you go.

Getting there/home If exiting Monument station by Fish Street Hill, turn right and the Monument is in front of you. If exiting by King William Street, turn left and take the first left, where the Monument will be visible. Having visited the museum, you will have a choice of stations for your return journey: Barbican (Metropolitan/Circle/ Hammersmith & City) in Aldersgate Street or St Paul's (Central Line).
Length of walk 1¼ miles. You can shorten the route by walking up St Martin Le Grand to the museum instead of going via West Smithfield, but you will miss Pye Corner.
Time 1 hour plus – and any length of time can be spent in the museum.
Terrain Pavement. Suitable for pushchairs. Access by lift to the museum.
Start The Monument, at the junction of Monument Street and Fish Street Hill.
Munch stop There is a fast food outlet in Cannon Street about 2 minutes from the Monument, which also has baby changing and toilets. Cafés are in abundance but some in the City are closed at the weekend. There is a supermarket next to Paternoster Square, a café in West Smithfield with toilets available in the square and the Museum of London has a picnic area, café and toilets. Whittington Garden (see point 2) would be a good place for a picnic en route.

The Walk

On the morning of 2nd September 1666 a fire started in a bakery belonging to Thomas Farynor, the King's baker, in Pudding Lane, just east of the ***Monument****. The fire raged across the City of London for*

Climb the steps inside the Monument for a great view over London

four days until the wind changed and the flames died down. Most of the buildings were made of wood so the fire was difficult to stop and spread very fast. Many people left their homes and some even spent time on boats on the Thames. Buildings were knocked down to stop the spread of the fire. Legend says that the fire finally abated near Pye Corner (see point 6). One of the buildings that managed to survive the fire is the Tudor property that leads to St Bartholomew the Great church in Little Britain (see point 8). This now looks very out of place squashed between two modern buildings.

The ***Monument*** *stands 202 feet high, the distance from where the Fire of London started. There are 311 steep steps to climb to the top but the view is worthwhile. The website www.themonument.info gives details of opening times and charges.*

1 Leave the Monument on the right in Fish Street Hill and turn left into Eastcheap. Cross at the traffic lights; to your left is London Bridge. Continue forward into Cannon Street. As you walk, glance over and on the opposite side of the road, between St Swithens Lane and Salters Hall Court, you will find the London Stone behind an iron grille. Turn left into Dowgate Hill then cross over.

I-SPY

In the lower part of the wall at No 9, look for the original iron boot scrapers.

Turn second right into College Street.

Protected by a screen and railings, near to the floor at No 111 Cannon Street, you can find the ***London Stone****. There are several ideas as to its origin, but it is said to bring good luck to the City of London and shouldn't be removed.*

2 If you walk just a little way further down College Street, there is a plaque on the side of the Innholders Hall, a livery company, mentioning how the original building was destroyed in the Great Fire. This was where the fire devoured almost everything in its path. On your left opposite the church of St Michael is Whittington Garden – an ideal spot to have a rest or an early picnic – named in honour of one of the most famous Lord Mayors. The church of St Michael, Paternoster Royal, is known as the Dick Whittington church and has a stained glass window in his memory. Bear round the side of the church into College Hill and walk up on the right-hand side. As you reach the far end of the

church you will find a plaque where the house belonging to Dick Whittington once stood. Continue along, turning left into Cloak Lane. Turn right at the end of Cloak Lane onto a paved area. Walk a short way across and turn left into Cannon Street.

There are many livery companies in the City of London. They are known for their charitable work and each is associated with trades that our ancestors were taught.

***St Michael's** in College Street was destroyed by the Great Fire and rebuilt by Sir Christopher Wren. Richard (Dick) Whittington, four times Lord Mayor of London, was buried in the original church in 1423.*

3 Cross the road by the traffic lights, then cross the next set, which is Queen Victoria Street. Turn left into Queen Victoria Street and bear round to the right. Turn right into Bow Lane, which is cobbled. Glance to your right down Watling Street and see the statue of the Cordwainer.

A cordwainer was someone who made shoes and other items from soft leather. This name came from Córdoba, a place in Spain where the leather originated.

4 Before you reach the end of Bow Lane turn left down by St Mary Le Bow church into Bow churchyard. You will come into a paved square. Cross the churchyard and walk towards the main road. Turn left into Cheapside. Cross New Change at the traffic lights and you will see St Paul's tube station.

5 Turn slightly left and proceed into the grounds of St Paul's Cathedral. Keep St Paul's on your left until you come to the main entrance steps on your left at the front of the cathedral. Turning right, you walk towards Paternoster Square. Here is a display board giving some history of the square and gates. Go through the large wooden gates, under the stone arch and enter the square. Retrace your steps back through Temple Bar and into St Paul's churchyard. Here you can get a good view of St Paul's Cathedral. Take the first turning right into Ava Maria Lane leading into Warwick Lane. You will pass another livery company at Cutlers Hall.

I-SPY

Look at the ornate carvings depicting their trade.

Turn left at the end into Newgate Street.

St Paul's Cathedral, *designed by Sir Christopher Wren, is the fourth cathedral to be built on this site, the third having been destroyed by the 1666 fire. Luckily this one survived the bombing in the Second World War. St Paul's has many famous connections. Lady Diana Spencer and Prince Charles were married here in 1981 and Admiral Nelson is buried in the crypt. See the website www.stpauls.co.uk or ☎ 0207 246 8357 for details of admission.*

Temple Bar, *now sited at the entrance to Paternoster Square, was originally erected in 1650 to differentiate the boundary between the City of London and Westminster. Subsequently purchased and erected in Theobalds Park, Hertfordshire, it was there for some 100 years. It is now back where it belongs in London.*

6 A little way down on the left is the Old Bailey, once Newgate Prison. At this point cross the road and walk down Giltspur Street at the side of the Viaduct Tavern. Continue down Giltspur Street and, as you look across the road to Cock Lane, you will notice a small statue of the Golden Boy in the side of the building. It is said that this is where the Fire of London finished at Pye Corner.

Newgate Prison *was destroyed in the Great Fire but was rebuilt in 1672 and again in 1780. Conditions inside the prison were appalling and Charles Dickens visited it and mentions it in several of his books, including* Oliver Twist. *It was demolished in 1902 and replaced with the Central Criminal Court, or Old Bailey as it is widely known.*

The first ***Metropolitan drinking fountain****, built in 1859, can now be found in the railings outside* ***St Sepulchre's church*** *on the corner at Giltspur Street, complete with metal drinking cups. This was a very popular place to drink clean water at a time when water generally wasn't safe. St Sepulchre's church is known for the twelve bells in the tower that are mentioned in the nursery rhyme 'Oranges and lemons', as 'When will you pay me, say the bells of Old Bailey'.*

The ***Golden Boy statue****, also known as 'The Fat Boy' stands with his arms folded over his tummy and is associated with gluttony because some people believed that the Great Fire was God's way of punishing Londoners for being greedy.*

7 Enter West Smithfield and look out for the only statue of King Henry the VIII in London, which is above the doorway at

The historic Temple Bar monument, with Paternoster Square behind

St Bartholomew's Hospital (it is thought he actually modelled for it). Continue along the side of the building and notice that there are large chunks missing from the wall – the damage from shrapnel during the Second World War.

8 Turn right into Little Britain where you can see a small Tudor gateway that was once the entrance to St Bartholomew the Great church. It was lucky to survive the Great Fire and now leads to a graveyard. Turn left into Montague Street. You can access the Museum of London from here via the Highwalk, which is signposted. You have now reached the end of the walk.

The ***Museum of London*** *is free to visit. Some of the exciting things you will find inside include a piece of the original Roman London wall, information about the Great Fire, remains of prehistoric animals and displays of what life was like in London hundreds of years ago. There are family events at weekends and exhibitions to keep the children amused whilst they learn about our fabulous city in a fun and imaginative way. For more details visit the website www.museumoflondon.org.uk or ☎ 020 7001 9844.*

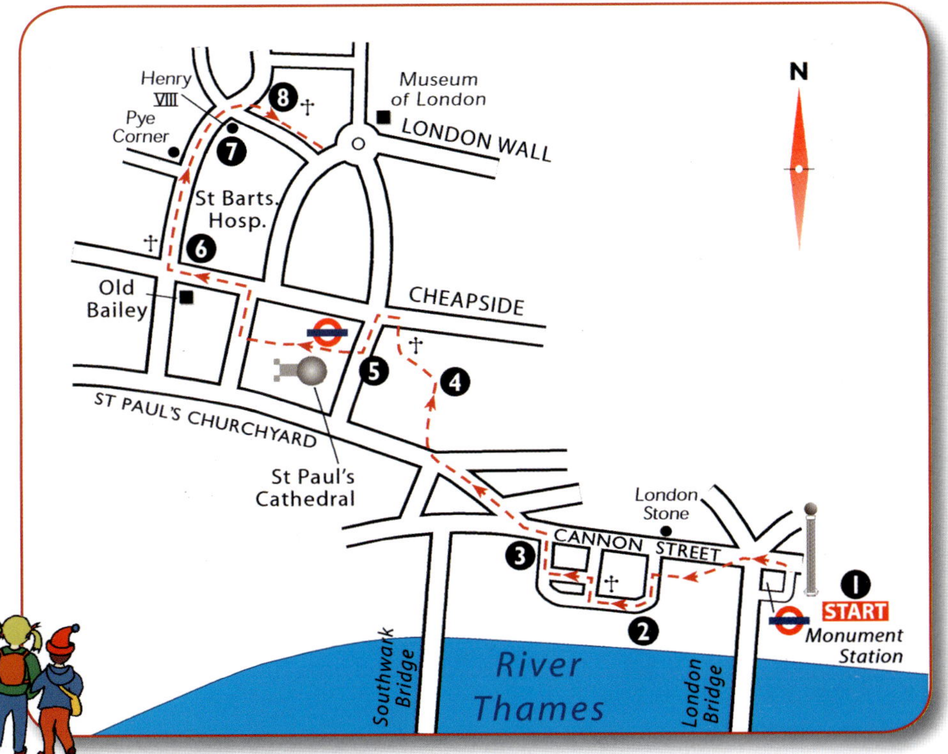

11

The Tower of London to the Millennium Bridge

A River Ramble

The magnificent Tower Bridge

This walk includes several famous landmarks. Starting at Trinity Square Gardens with its nautical memorials and next to a great castle, the Tower of London, it continues across Tower Bridge to the south side and Potters Fields for a munch break and run about. After you have imagined life on the high seas on board a large Tudor ship, the *Golden Hinde*, a cobbled street transports you back in time on land – but behave yourselves, the Clink Prison is nearby. A little further on and Shakespeare's Globe Theatre stands proudly alongside the Thames – a living memorial to a literary genius. Then there is the Tate Modern gallery in the former Bankside power station building, before the Millennium Bridge, opened for general use in 2002, takes you back across the river. This varied route brings old and new – historic London and the 21st century – together in a remarkably vivid way.

The Tower of London to the Millennium Bridge

Getting there/ home Tower Hill station, alongside Trinity Square Gardens, is on the District/Circle line. St Paul's station (Central line) is easily reached from the end of the Millennium Bridge for your return journey.
Length of walk 1–2 miles.
Time 2 hours plus.
Terrain Difficult for pushchairs unless you can carry them or have a child back-carrier as there are steps up and down in places.
Start Trinity Square Gardens.
Munch stop There are various food outlets en route and several picnic opportunities. Toilets are on the right-hand side next to the cafés opposite the Tower of London. The Tate Modern has a café and toilets.

The Walk

1 Walk into Trinity Square Gardens with its anchor in the centre and memorials for seamen. Here is somewhere you can have a sit down, picnic or a munch stop. There is plenty of room for the children to let off some steam after travelling.

I-SPY

Can you see the dolphin plant holder?

The building behind the park is Trinity House, a Port of London Authority building.

I-SPY

Can you see some ships in the architecture and the monument of Neptune?

In Trinity Square Gardens you can go down the steps and see more memorials. Passing by the statues of a fisherman and Merchant Navy seaman, you will notice many names carved.

I-SPY

Can you spot a tile on the wall with five seahorses in it?

Trinity Square Gardens *has many monuments and statues for us to remember seamen who have lost their lives during both World Wars and the Falklands War. Their resting place is the sea.*

2 Return to street level and exit onto Tower Hill, opposite the Tower of London. Just on the right you can see All Hallows by the Tower, the oldest church in the City. Cross over and onto the paved area, keeping the Tower of London on your left, and continue walking towards the River Thames.

Look out for the Beefeaters in their bright red uniforms.

Turn left, walking along the cobbled path beside the Tower towards Tower Bridge.

As you walk, look up on the side of the tower and find a crown on the weather vane.

Pass Traitors' Gate.

Imagine what it would have been like arriving by boat, coming through and climbing the few steps, knowing that you might never leave this castle prison. Can you see any unusual gargoyles positioned around the Tower?

Walk past the cannons, through the archway and tunnel via Dead Man's Hole up onto the bridge.

The Tower of London *is probably one of the capital's most famous landmarks. Building started not long after 1066 when William the Conqueror came to England. Having been used as a palace and a prison, amongst other things, it has been witness to many an execution. Two of Henry VIII's wives, Anne Boleyn and Kathryn Howard, were beheaded here. The Beefeaters, or Yeoman Warders, can be recognised by their traditional red and black tunics and black hats. Their duties include keeping the tourists happy whilst watching over the ravens, whose ancestors have been at the Tower for hundreds of years. It is believed that if the ravens ever leave the Tower, London will fall. The Crown Jewels are also stored here and the crown that the Queen uses for the State Opening of Parliament is removed for that occasion. There is a gift shop, which can be visited without entering the Tower of London, along with an information centre. You will find plenty of places to sit alongside the Thames, with great views over the water and the fantastic backdrop of this famous London castle.*

3 Continue across Tower Bridge and turn right at the end. Follow the Thames Path/Queen's Walk signs. On the left is Potters Fields, where you can choose to picnic or the children can have a run about. Continue under London Bridge.

The Tower of London to the Millennium Bridge

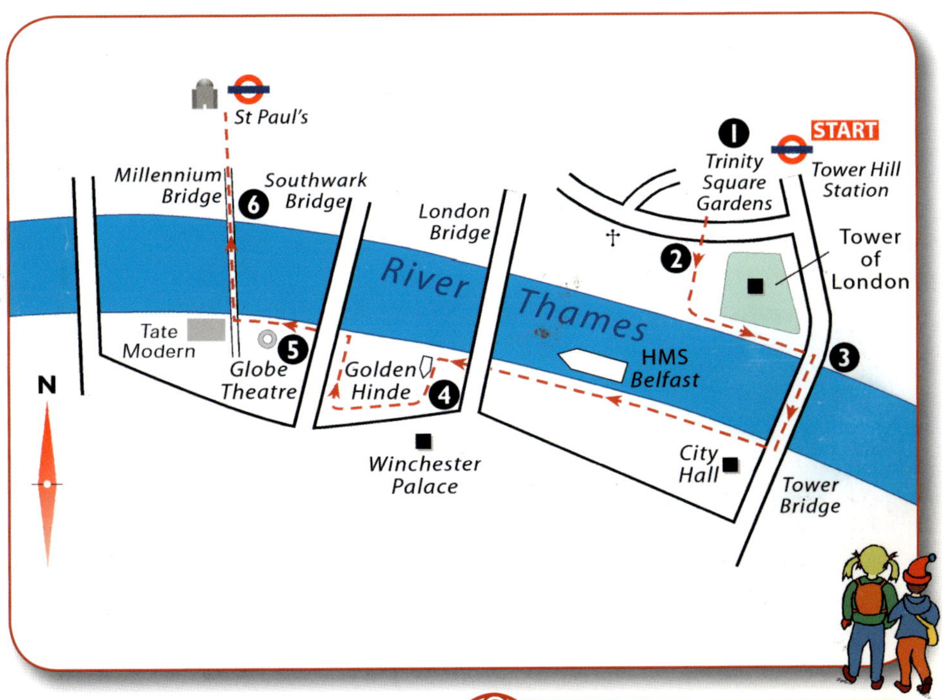

The magnificent ***Tower Bridge*** *was opened in 1894. It has a museum inside (details from www.towerbridge.org.uk) and you can learn about its history and how the bridge was constructed.*

4 Signs divert you away from the river slightly via the replica of the *Golden Hinde*. You continue along and then follow the cobbled stones in Clink Street, passing the remains of Winchester Palace, the one-time London home of the Bishops of Winchester.

I-SPY

Look up and find the rose window.

Continue along Clink Street, with the museum on your left, and turn right into Bank End. Rejoin the path alongside the Thames again and go under Southwark Bridge.

The ***Golden Hinde*** *is a full size replica of the Tudor ship used by Sir Francis Drake to circumnavigate the world between 1577 and 1580. This is now a floating museum. They hold* *special events so it is worth checking the website www.goldenhinde.com.*

The ***Clink Prison Museum*** *stands today on the original site of the Clink gaol. It was used for prisoners from 1151 until 1780 when it was burnt down and never rebuilt. Its name, which is said to have come from the 'clinking' of metal on the doors or from the chains the prisoners wore, is now recalled by the phrase 'in the Clink', referring to being in prison.*

5 On your left is Shakespeare's Globe Theatre. To the right of the theatre there are some very old houses. Christopher Wren once lived here. At Bankside you are in front of the Tate Modern art gallery. You need to go up the slope and onto the Millennium Bridge. This affords a good view of the Thames and towering over you as you walk across is St Paul's Cathedral.

The original ***Globe Theatre*** *was built along the Thames in 1597 and many of William Shakespeare's plays were performed there. Sam Wanamaker, an American film director and actor (father to Zoë Wanamaker, who played Madam Hooch in* Harry Potter and the Philosopher's Stone*), was dismayed to find that there was no memorial to such a famous writer and he decided to have a replacement built. It was many years before his plan for the new Globe Theatre was realised. Building started in 1993 but unfortunately Sam Wanamaker died before it was completed in 1997. It is constructed in the same style as the original, with an open roof. Plays are performed here throughout the summer, with many of the audience standing as 'groundlings', as they would have done in Shakespeare's time.*

The ***Tate Modern*** *is an art gallery with a difference. Not to be confused with the Tate Gallery in Millbank, it displays various forms of modern art, including some unconventional structures and designs.*

Millennium Bridge*, or the Wobbly Bridge as it is known, was built to mark the new Millennium in 2000. Only a couple of days after opening it had to be closed for reinforcement as it 'swayed' too much when the crowds of pedestrians walked across, and was reopened for public use two years later. This conveniently placed footbridge brings the north and south of the river together.*

6 Walk straight ahead along Peter's Hill, cross over Queen Victoria Street at the traffic lights and continue until you reach

St Paul's churchyard. Turn right, then left up New Change and St Paul's underground station is on the corner.

The Golden Hinde, a replica of the ship used by Sir Francis Drake

12

Mudchute Farm

Out and About with the Animals

Mudchute – Europe's largest city farm

The **wonderful Mudchute Farm** on the Isle of Dogs, at 32 acres, is the largest city farm in London. There are around 200 animals and birds to be seen here, some free-roaming and others in pens, and many rare breeds. The nearby park can be visited all day, every day and the farm itself is open from Tuesday to Sunday throughout the year – with free entry to both. It is a versatile place for family outings and you can spend as long as you want here and take different routes to suit your own interests. The maps situated around the park are very clear and self-explanatory. Depending on what pastures and enclosures the farm is using, there could be different animals in them each time you visit. Although we didn't extend this walk, as there was enough enjoyment here, you can continue into Millwall Park, signposted to the south, which has a play area. Continue walking towards the river and you will get a good view across to the Royal Naval College, Greenwich.

Getting there The nearest station is Mudchute on the Docklands Light Railway. The Greenwich Foot Tunnel is nearby if you want to combine a visit to Mudchute Farm with Walk 13; you can then return on the DLR from Cutty Sark. The distance from the farm to Greenwich is approximately ¾ mile. Bear in mind, though, that there are steps in and out of the tunnel and although there is a lift at the tunnel, it is not always in operation.
Length of walk 1 mile – you can shorten or lengthen the walk depending on how much time you want to spend there.
Time 2 hours plus.
Terrain Suitable for pushchairs and wheelchairs. NB: footwear should be appropriate for farm/park walking.
Start Mudchute station.
Munch stop The farm has a café serving a variety of good food, with a picnic area and toilets alongside. There is also a superstore further along East Ferry Road.

The Walk

Please note *that if you are pregnant you should not enter the lambing pens. There are signs reminding visitors to wash their hands and facilities can be found near the café and information area. If you have any questions or concerns, the rangers and staff will be very happy to assist.*

1 Exit Mudchute station, cross the road and turn left. Enter Mudchute Park by the gate. You will see a plan of the park here. Casting your eye over to the left you will see a block of flats but also the spikes of the O2 Dome. You can even get a good view of Canary Wharf. Walk up the steps and reach the stone circular pavement area. Bear to the right and join the bridleway.

I-SPY

You may see some horses along here. Look out for the sheep walking freely and if you glance up you may see aeroplanes that are to-ing and fro-ing from City Airport.

Where ***Mudchute Farm and Park*** *now stand was originally derelict land created from the spoil resulting*

12

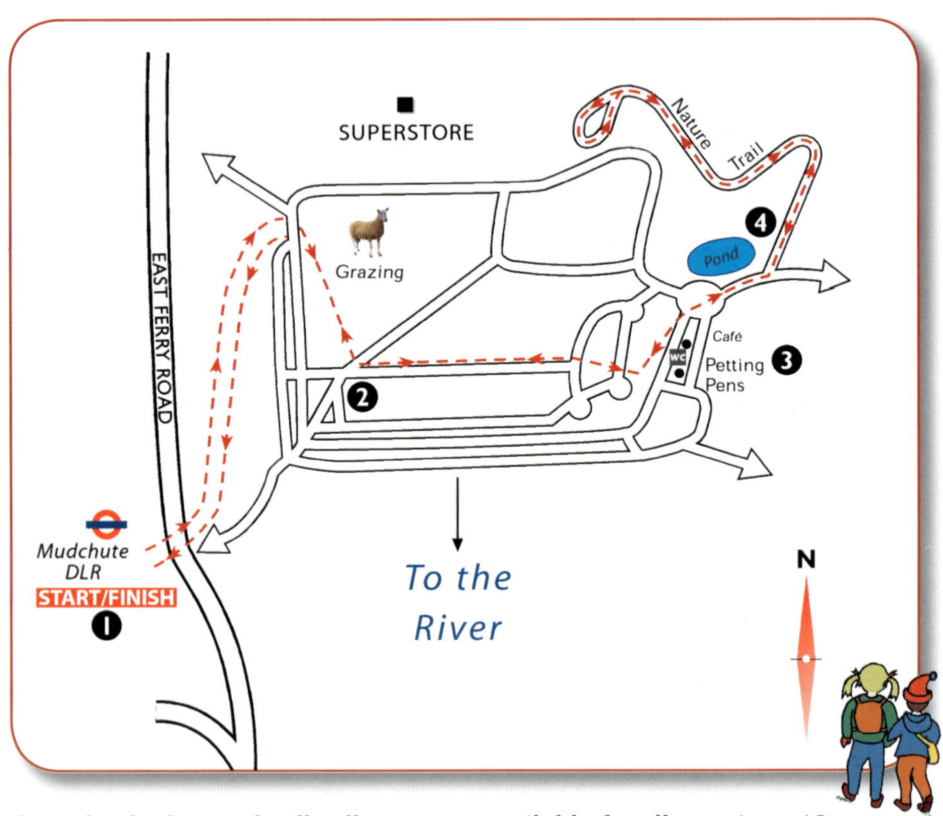

from the dredging of Millwall Dock. It was left unattended for many years, with flora and fauna flourishing. When, in 1974, the Greater London Council decided to build a high-rise estate on the land, the local people were very opposed to the plans. Thankfully the public won and were able to keep the area in its natural state, known as the 'People's Park'. What you see today is an inner city farm with happy and well looked after animals that is available for all to enjoy – 'Country life in the heart of East London', as the website says – as well as a conservation project and a natural habitat. For further details see the website www.mudchute.org or ☎ 020 7515 5901.

2 Keep on the bridleway and look for the directions to the café. Enter the courtyard and you will see the café and picnic areas with plenty of seating. Here you

will also find toilets and hand-washing facilities.

*The café – **Mudchute Kitchen** – has some inside seating, including a couple of sofas, and some toys for young children to play with. They serve delicious home-made food. There is something to tempt all taste buds. Hot meals are available, as well as snacks, and the most delightful and unusual cakes and*

fresh juices. They have their own allotment for fresh produce, and also sell jams and preserves.

3 Walk through the archway on the left and you will come to the small animal area. A turkey or two may greet you but they will run away if approached. There are many signs asking children not to chase the animals and birds, so please bear this in mind if you have very young children. Here you will find budgies, rabbits, guinea pigs and interesting facts about all the different types of animals.

I-SPY

Have a look and see if any of the chickens are digging holes to lay their eggs in. Did you know that the chicken is the closest living relative we have to the tyrannosaurus? And did you know that turkeys were introduced to England in 1524? See if you can find out what different names of a male, female and baby turkey are. (Don't mention Christmas Dinner!)

4 Leave the café area and follow the directions to the pond and nature walk. Usually home to various ducks and geese, the pond is sometimes left for frogs to develop. If this is the case you may find the birds in the pens opposite (to avoid the spawn being a tasty treat for a duck or goose).

I-SPY

Can you find the goose with the big black bump on his head?

If you see a ranger they are very happy to assist with any questions you may have regarding the species of any of the animals.

5 Continue walking along the nature trail, keeping the pond on your left. Bear round to the left. When you have reached the end, you could try to get through but it is safer to loop back the same way. Back at the ducks, you can either explore the park more at your leisure and visit the different pens housing llamas, pigs, goats and other animals and birds, or return along the bridleway. You can also cut across the meadow area, containing the free roaming sheep. Return down the steps to the gate where you came in. Turn left, cross the road and you are back at Mudchute DLR station.

13

The Thames and Maritime Greenwich

Nautical but Nice

The Royal Naval College seen from the river

The best way to approach this walk at Greenwich is to begin at Westminster Pier and travel along the Thames at a leisurely pace by river cruise. Normally the Captain and crew are very good at pointing out places of interest en route. It also gives a good view of buildings along the Thames that might not be seen on foot. On arrival at Greenwich Pier you get a feel of how Henry VIII or Sir Walter Raleigh would have approached when the original Greenwich Palace stood here. This circular walk, crammed full with interesting sights, takes you to the Old Royal Naval College, the National Maritime Museum and the Royal Observatory. The new 'Discover Greenwich' centre houses displays about the area. As you wander through the park up to the Meridian Line you get a great view over London. If the children have any energy left after all this, there is a playground in the park.

Getting there If you are taking the boat trip to Greenwich, start at Westminster Pier (close to Westminster tube station); sometimes reductions/offers are available if you have an underground ticket. There are several river cruise operators – (see www.citycruises.com or www.thamesriverservices.co.uk). Alternatively, travel direct by Docklands Light Railway to Cutty Sark for Maritime Greenwich.
Length of walk Approximately 1 mile (not including boat trip).
Time 2 hours at least, plus the river trip which takes approximately 1¼ hours. You could spend anything up to a full day if you want to try and pack in visits to the museum and the Royal Observatory at the same time.
Terrain Tarmac/pathways and grass in park. Suitable for all (although a steep walk if you visit the Meridian Line and Royal Observatory).
Start Westminster Pier for the river cruise; the riverside entrance to the Old Royal Naval College for the walk itself.
Munch stop Picnic in Greenwich Park. There are toilets in the National Maritime Museum. The Discover Greenwich centre in the Old Royal Naval College has a café and toilets.

The Walk

The maps for Walks 7, 8, 9 and 11 may be useful for identifying some of the sights you may see from the boat.

1 All aboard at Westminster Pier. As you leave Big Ben and the statue of Boudicca behind (see Walk 8), you will see many of London's famous sights. The first

is a great view of the London Eye. On the left there is Cleopatra's Needle.

I-SPY

Look out for the amphibious tour boat on the Thames. It travels on the river and the road. Imagine that you are travelling down the river 200 years ago. You would probably have been stuck in a long traffic jam full of ships of all shapes and sizes; each carrying different goods from wood to wool, silk to slaves, tea, fruit, ice and spices.

On the left just after Waterloo Bridge, you will see several ships. One is the HQS *Wellington*, this is the only floating livery hall. On the right is the Oxo Tower.

***HQS* Wellington** *has been moored in London since 1948 when she participated in the Second World War. The only floating livery company (see Walk 10 for other livery companies), she is home to the Master Mariners and the Hackney Carriage Drivers who represent the London taxi trade.*

As you approach Blackfriars Bridge look to see the original pillars of the old railway bridge. After Blackfriars Bridge you will notice on the right the Tate Modern art gallery and on the left a view of St Paul's Cathedral. As you sail under the Millennium Bridge on your right you can see Shakespeare's Globe Theatre. The next bridge is Southwark Bridge. You will then get a glimpse of the

Shakespeare's Globe Theatre

Golden Hinde on the right. London Bridge is next (hopefully not falling down). The large battleship you will see is HMS *Belfast*.

Part of the collection of the Imperial War Museum, **HMS Belfast** *was one of the most powerful large cruisers of its day. She is the only surviving one of this type that actually participated in the Second World War. Saved from the scrapyard after her duties were over, she has been moored in London since 1971 for all to enjoy. Special events and various exhibitions are arranged to encourage children to learn about life onboard a ship.*

From now on keep an eye out for the original wharves and landing areas where the goods would have been delivered. If you look on the south side of the river, you may even see some of the cranes on the sides of buildings that were used to haul up the goods from the ships.

Pass the original building of Old Billingsgate Market on the left and then watch for the unusual shape of City Hall (where the Mayor of London works) on the right. On the left the Tower of London looms into view. Look down towards the river edge and notice the entrance to Traitors' Gate. Imagine being taken through Traitors' Gate, never to return.

Sail under Tower Bridge and you will notice the wharves now converted into luxury apartments. Arriving at Greenwich Pier you get a very good idea of what it must have been like for anyone approaching from the river to visit this palace. Alight here to continue the walk on dry land.

Originally called the Palace of Placentia, **Greenwich Palace** *was the birthplace of Henry VIII in 1491 and his daughters, Queen Mary (1516) and Elizabeth I (1533), and was his main place of residence during his marriages to Catherine of Aragon and Anne Boleyn. It was while Elizabeth I lived here as Queen that she gave orders for her fleet of ships to go to fight in the Spanish Armada. After the palace was demolished it was rebuilt as the Greenwich Hospital in 1694, later becoming the Royal Naval Hospital.*

2 Walk towards the entrance of the Old Royal Naval College.

I-SPY

Can you see a crown on a lamppost? Pause to read the plaque in the paving. What famous people were born here?

Admiring HMS Belfast

Continue ahead. Stop off at the various places of interest on the way up such as the Painted Hall on the right. Cross the Romney Road, continuing towards the signs for the National Maritime Museum.

A crown on top of a lamppost

I-SPY

Look out for the large anchor.

Spend some time here wandering through the various exhibits.

*The original design for the **Old Royal Naval College** (Royal Naval Hospital) was by Sir Christopher Wren, but various other architects completed it. Initially built to give help to seamen and their relatives, it was also used as a naval hospital. It closed in 1869 when the number of patients declined. It was then used as a training college for officers and is now run by a charitable foundation. The Painted Hall is a wonderful place to visit. Looking up* *at the ceiling, you can understand how it took the painter, Sir James Thornhill, 19 years to complete. It is worth sparing time to examine the detail in the paintings. Originally the dining room, it is still used today for special events. Admiral Lord Nelson's body lay in state here before it was moved upriver to St Paul's Cathedral where he is buried. Entry is free, although you can pay to join a guided tour (no charge for the under 16s); the website www.oldroyalnavalcollege.org gives details.*

Entry to the ***National Maritime Museum*** *is free too – the website www.nmm.ac.uk gives further information. Among so much that is of interest here, there are exhibits relating to Nelson and the Battle of Trafalgar.*

❸ Continue round the back of the building, passing the statue of Captain Cook, following the signs for Greenwich Park and the Observatory. Walk along the main pathway, Jubilee Avenue, all the way up to the Royal Observatory and the Meridian Line. After having a photo taken with one foot in the western hemisphere and one in the eastern hemisphere you can take a look at the weights and measures on the wall.

The ***Royal Observatory*** *is a museum containing information about astronomy and navigational instruments, as well as the history of time-keeping for ships. It was founded at the time of King Charles II. Look for the time ball on the top. At 12.55 pm every day, it moves halfway up the pole, reaching the top at 12.58 pm. At 1 pm it drops. Ships on the Thames have used this method of time-keeping for many years as it can be seen from the river. The Planetarium nearby houses information about space travel so would be interesting to any budding astronauts!*

The ***Meridian Line*** *is an imaginary line running from the North Pole to the South Pole. It is where time is measured from at Greenwich, 'GMT' standing for Greenwich Mean Time.*

❹ Retrace your steps back on the grass and cut across at a diagonal to the right towards the children's playground. There is plenty of room in the park for a picnic.

❺ Walk left as you leave the play area, towards the sundial. Continue along that path and leave the park at St Mary's Gate in the right-hand corner. This leads into King William Walk. Cross Nelson Road and continue

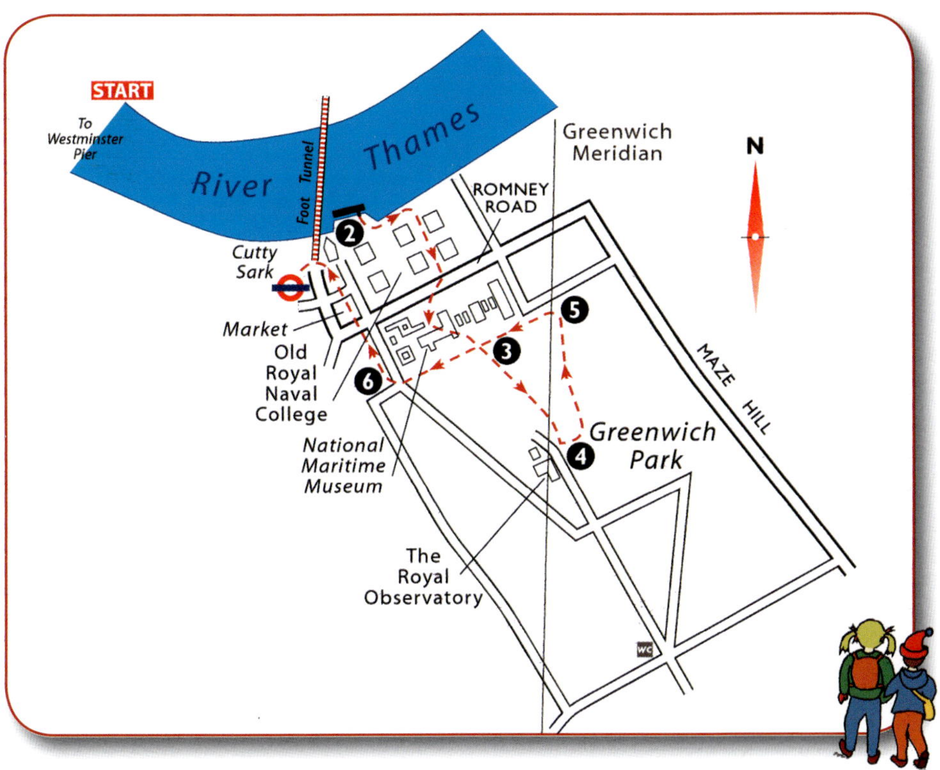

until you reach Greenwich Market on your left. Cross over and enter the market. There are various stalls here and some quaint shops including an old-fashioned sweet shop. Walk through the market and exit into College Approach. Cross the road and turn left. Cutty Sark DLR station is on the corner. If you have time, you may want to visit the *Cutty Sark*. This is signposted from here and is only a few minutes away.

Built in 1869 to be the fastest ship on the China Tea Run, the **Cutty Sark** *is the only surviving tea clipper. She has 11 miles of rigging and 34 sails. At the time of writing, she is undergoing a major renovation. This conservation will enable her to last for many more years to come. It is well worth visiting to get a feel of what it must have been like with no engine and only sails to get through the most treacherous of seas safely. The website www.cuttysark.org.uk gives details.*

14

Woodlands Farm and Oxleas Wood

'Wood' You Like to Wander?

Meeting one of the residents at Woodlands Farm

Woodlands Farm and Oxleas Wood

Whatever time of year you decide to visit, this is a lovely relaxing walk that is complemented by every season. Woodlands Farm is run by a charitable trust with the aim of balancing farming practice with nature conservation and is a fascinating place for children to get close to farm animals. Oxleas Wood, one of the last remaining ancient deciduous forests in the area, gives plenty of opportunities for youngsters to run around, collect leaves, play hide and seek and learn about the different trees. You can choose to visit Woodlands Farm or Oxleas Wood independently but you can easily fit them both in half a day. It is well worth extending the walk to look at Severndroog Castle, if you have time. Although it is in a state of disrepair at present, the Friends of Severndroog are in the process of raising funds to restore it to its former glory.

Getting there The Oxleas Wood free car park in Crown Woods Lane is on the south side of Shooters Hill, the A207, to the east of its junction with the A205. Bus routes 89 and 486 stop outside the farm.
Length of walk Approximately 1½ miles.
Time Up to an hour walking (plus the farm visit). There are plenty of places to stop for munch breaks and games too.
Terrain Tarmac pathways in part but wellies may be needed in the woods and farm, depending on the time of year. Suitable for pushchairs.
Start The car park in Crown Woods Lane, or the entrance to Woodlands Farm (see point 2) if you come by bus.
Munch stop There is a picnic area at the farm, as well as informal places to stop in the woods. A café alongside the car park in Oxleas Wood serves a great variety of food and drinks. Toilets are at the farm and next to the café.

The Walk

1 From the car park in Crown Woods Lane, walk back the way you came in. Cross Shooters Hill Road at the crossing and turn right. You will see the water tower on your left. Continue along and Woodlands Farm entrance is on the left (approximately 10 minutes from the car park).

14

__Shooters Hill Road__ was originally part of the Roman road to Dover on the coast of Kent. At its summit which on starting the walk is back towards the left as you cross the road (432 ft/132 m) Shooters Hill is one of the highest points in Greater London. It is thought that the name may have come either from the highwaymen who frequented the area in the days of Dick Turpin or from the practising of archery here in the Middle Ages. The water tower, which is very ornate, was built in 1910 and is still in use. Water is pumped here from chalk wells at Orpington and falls by gravity to the pumping station in Well Hall Road.

2 Turn into the farm. The animals change pens sometimes so it is best to follow the signs within the farm.

I-SPY

You may see Shetland ponies, ducks, donkeys, sheep and various other animals. Listen out for the wild birds. You may even hear a woodpecker tapping away.

Continue through the farm and you will find old tractors, a pond and a picnic area.

In 1997 __Woodlands Farm__ was saved from the threat of housing development to be run as a community farm working on conservation principles. Set in 89 acres, it is open from Tuesday to Sunday throughout the year and entry is free. Lamb, honey and eggs are for sale. Educational activities are arranged for school visits and lots of events of interest to children are held here. The website www.thewoodlandsfarmtrust.org will provide you with up-to-date information.

3 When you have finished your visit, return to the main road and turn left. Continue along the main road. Before you reach the garage and pub, cross over and you will see the entrance to Oxleas Wood just before the first house. This is part of the Green Chain Walk. Walk through the woods, bearing to the right and following the path. There are arrows on signposts indicating the direction. Pass the split tree, which is great for a photo.

I-SPY

Watch out for the tree roots running across the paths.

Over 8,000 years old, __Oxleas Wood__ is now a Site of Special Scientific Interest and a Local Nature Reserve. Here you will find oak trees, silver birch, hornbeam and coppice hazel, sheltering many different species of birds. There are various toadstools to be seen too, in the autumn.

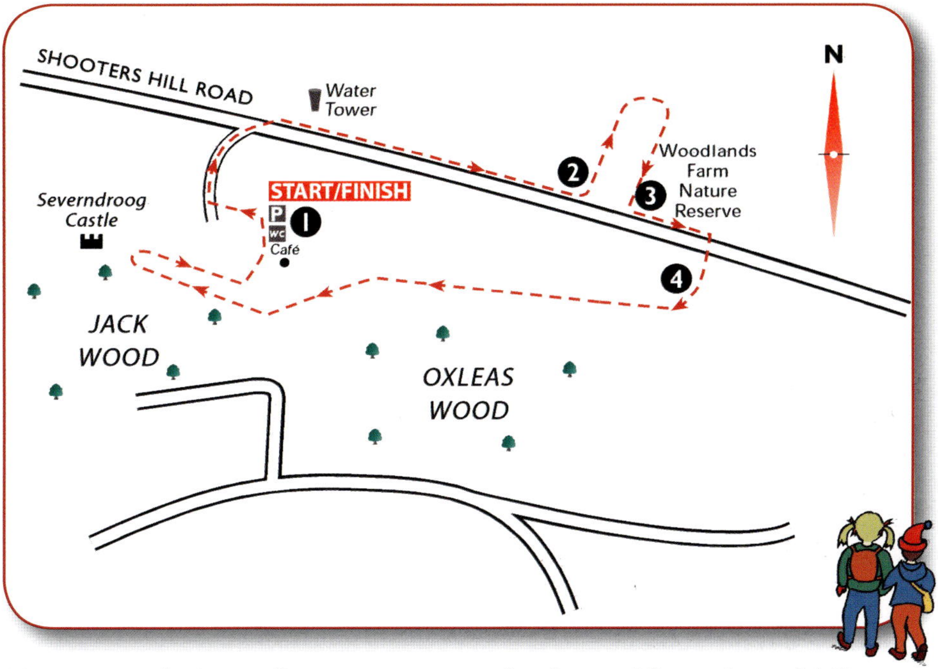

Woodlands Farm and Oxleas Wood

SHOOTERS HILL ROAD
Water Tower
N
Woodlands Farm Nature Reserve
START/FINISH
P
WC
Café
Severndroog Castle
JACK WOOD
OXLEAS WOOD

*The **Green Chain Walks** cover south-east London and link the green spaces to be found in this area of London and reach out to parts of Kent. They can be walked in part or whole. Visit www.greenchain.com for further information.*

Continue along the path.

If you look carefully to the side of the path, you may see different types of toadstools. Please don't pick these. See if you can find the largest.

Take the middle path and follow the directions towards the café.

4 Continue straight on at the crossroads and have a rest on the bench. Turn right at the end and follow the tree-lined path round to the right. To your left across the field you can get a good view on a clear day over towards Crystal Palace and see the communications mast. This is a good place to stop for a munch break or to play a game. The path is now slightly uphill and at the top you will see the café. You can choose to end the walk

14

The forlorn Severndroog Castle

With a name sounding like something out of an adventure story, the Gothic-looking **Severndroog Castle** *was built in 1784 as a memorial to Sir William James by his wife, Lady James. It was to commemorate his most memorable expedition, in 1755, when he defeated pirates off the west coast of India. The Severndroog Castle Building Preservation Trust has been formed and has plans to renovate the building if enough money can be raised. The site at www.severndroogcastle.org.uk gives up-to-date information on the restoration project and fundraising; plans for the future include a viewing platform and café, as well as a castle history.*

When you've finished having a look around, continue back down the hill and carefully down the steps into the rose garden. Have a rest on the benches here. On a clear day you will have a fantastic view over London. Return the way you came, back to the café and car park.

here as the car park is just on the right.

If you want to continue to Severndroog Castle, follow the signs indicated on the map outside the café. The path is slightly uneven and takes approximately 10–15 minutes. Watch out for green parakeets flying above.